LET'S CELEBRATE GROWTH AND LIFE. L'CHAIM!

"עֵץ חַיִּים הִיא לַמַּחֲזִיקִים בָּהּ וְתֹמְכֶיהָ מְאֻשָּׁר"

She is a tree of life to those who hold fast to HER, and those who support HER are fortunate.
(Mishlei 3:18)

This verse teaches that Torah is a living source of life and nourishment.
When we hold it close and support it, it sustains us, grounds us,
and allows us to grow.

Something about the season feels especially alive.
Like *Tu B'Shvat*, it invites us to plant and trust what is quietly growing
beneath the surface. With *Adar* upon us and *Purim* approaching, the air feels
lighter, a reminder that joy expands the heart, loosens what feels heavy,
and gently turns things around, *V'nahafoch Hu.*
This edition was created in that spirit.

Her Tribe. You are HER. She is you.

Women from all walks of life, across generations, sharing meaningful moments.
When our stories meet, our roots grow stronger.

Her Tribe magazine grows because of you. Your presence, your thoughts, your
honesty, and your kindness shape what Her Tribe becomes.

This edition is also a shared celebration. **One year of Her Tribe**, six wonderful
editons and a personal milestone for me as well: my birthday which falls during
Parshat Beshalach.
A *parsha* of *geula* and *emuna*. Of sisterhood, courage, and song.
Perhaps that explains a little why this magazine exists and what lives at its core.
So instead of cakes and big speeches, I want to offer you a *bracha.*
Heart to heart. *Neshama* to *neshama.*

May we continue to grow with patience and joy.
May we gently release what no longer serves us and reveal who we truly are.
May our homes be filled with *shalom bayit*, our days with *simcha*, our bodies with
briut.
And may we feel deeply connected to ourselves,
Hashem, to one another,
and to *Am Yisrael.*

P.S. Make my day and send me your Hebrew
name and your mother's Hebrew name so I can
daven for your hatzlacha:
hello@hertribemagazine.com
Subject: *Mazal tov to us!*

Naomi Journo &
The Team

Shvat שְׁבָט

ROOTS, GROWTH, AND THE WISDOM OF THE TREES

By Yaffa Palti

ART "TREE POSE" BY SHEVA CHAYA | SHEVACHAYA.COM

So apparently, I'm supposed to write about trees, *Shvat*, growth, and renewal. And that's exactly why *Shvat* doesn't wait for spring. Which sounds inspiring.

Except it's winter.
Everything looks dead.
And if we're being honest, some of us feel that way too, emotionally, spiritually, or because starting anything right now feels like a lot.

And that's exactly why *Shvat* doesn't wait for spring.

THE TORAH SAYS, "KI HA'ADAM ETZ HASADEH,"

A person is like a tree.
Comforting… and mildly inconvenient. Because trees don't rush. They don't panic in January wondering where their leaves went or why everyone else looks more together. They just stand there, bare, quiet, unimpressive, while everything important is happening underground.

Here's what we forget every winter: the sap is already rising. You can't see it, measure it, or put it on a vision board, but it's happening. And so is your growth. This time of year, I hear women say, "Nothing is changing,"

or "I'm trying so hard," or "I should be better by now."
Let me translate that into real life.

You're staring at piles of clean laundry on the couch, which you affectionately named Mount Washmore, and thinking, This is my life now.
I know, because I've been there.
Clean clothes. Good intentions.
Zero system. Until one day, not dramatically, not magically,
I discovered laundry baskets.

And then, slowly, one sock at a time (literally, because I couldn't find the other one), a system was born.
Nothing changed overnight.
But something shifted.
That's how growth works.

Trees deepen roots first. Sometimes growth moves downward before it ever moves up.

Take patience, for example. Have you ever decided you're going to "work on it"? Very noble, until five minutes later someone spills, loses, argues, or asks the question you answered thirty seconds ago. And you think, Great. I'm failing.

Except you're not.

Growth doesn't always look like instant calm. Sometimes it looks like catching yourself one second sooner, pausing before reacting, or apologizing afterward, which, by the way, also counts as growth. And sometimes growth looks like realizing the conversation you fully resolved in your head was never actually shared with your husband.
Also growth.

Shvat reminds us of something else we forget when we're busy judging ourselves: we're not meant to grow alone. We're one people, one root system, different branches, different directions, still deeply connected.

And sometimes growth doesn't look like standing tall and independent. Sometimes it looks like leaning. There are trees that remain standing only because another tree is holding them up.

Which makes me wonder how many women around us are holding more than we realize. Sometimes real support looks less like advice and more like sitting together, sharing warmth, and not trying to fix a thing.
And then there's pruning. No one loves this part.

But pruning isn't punishment, it's maintenance. Letting go of draining habits, old narratives, and unrealistic expectations isn't failure. It's how energy starts flowing again.
Tu B'Shvat reminds us to honor the process: hard shells, soft centers, sweetness that takes time.

So if it feels like winter in your life right now, emotionally, spiritually, or just in your living room, remember this: winter doesn't mean nothing is happening. It means something is happening.
The roots are strengthening. The sap is rising.

And can I just say, I've heard that phrase my whole life, and I'm still not sure anyone knows what sap is. But we do know it's essential. It carries nourishment upward long before anything beautiful shows up on the outside.

Sometimes growth is like that too, a little sticky, a little unglamorous, absolutely necessary. And eventually… sweet.

And if you're still living with Mount Washmore and mismatched socks, welcome! You're not failing. You're growing.

Just start where you are, one basket, one pause, one imperfect step.

Yaffa Palti is a Torah educator, international speaker, and singer-songwriter known for making Torah feel real, relatable, and deeply human. Through teaching, writing, and music, she empowers women to navigate life's emotional and spiritual seasons with warmth, clarity, and humor.

▶ Yaffa Palti Channel
⊙ @yaffapalti

ART 'TREE OF LIFE' BY SHEVA CHAYA | SHEVACHAYA.COM

אֲדָר

Adar: Expanding Joy Beyond the Surface

By Rebbetzin Yehudis Golshevsky

dar is not simply a happy month. It is a month of *simchah* but not the joy that comes when everything is easy. The potential of *Adar* reaches far deeper. It is joy that can expand into places where it does not usually live.

Each month carries its own inner quality, its own domain. Much of what we know about this comes from *Sefer Yetzirah*, where every month is linked to a letter, a faculty, and a part of the body. These are not symbols. They describe how spiritual energy moves through the world.

The organ associated with *Adar* is the spleen. In older language, the spleen represents irritation, being easily annoyed, splenetic. The *avodah* of *Adar* is the inversion of that state. Its quality is *sechok*, an inner playfulness, a freedom-born laughter.

This is not laughter at a joke. It is the laughter that arrives when the story suddenly opens and you realize it is not what you thought. A release from living under constant pressure and inner tightness.

Every person has a cellar. Not a pleasant basement, but a dark place where light rarely reaches and joy usually does not enter. Even when life is working, there is often a place that remains closed.

The *avodah* of *Adar* is that joy can reach even there.

Adar opens a window so *simchah* can enter places it normally cannot. That is why *Purim* appears the way it does. Boundaries loosen, not to create chaos, but to allow what has long been suppressed to emerge.

6

When restraint softens, what often comes forth is generosity, connection, and love.

Purim is not an easy story. It is a frightening one. And yet it becomes a story of reversal, *V'nahafoch Hu.* That is *Adar.*

From the outside, the Jewish people appeared divided and asleep. *Haman* saw only that surface. He did not see what lived within. Inside there was vitality, connection, something *adir* (awesome).

Adar often looks dark, cold, rainy and depleted. Yet inwardly it is full of life. The work is to be warm inside, even when the world feels frozen.

The letter of *Adar* is *kuf,* descending below the line. *Nissan's* letter is *hei,* revelation and clarity. *Adar* comes first.

It is the end of the cycle, and the preparation for what follows. Before revealed joy, there must be expanded joy. Before open miracles, inner vitality.

The joy of *Adar* does not depend on circumstance. It rests in knowing there is **no place** where *HaKadosh Baruch Hu* **is not present**, even in the cellar. This awareness is the *daat* of Moshe Rabbeinu. Every Jew carries a spark of it. Sharing a simple, real awareness of *Hashem* is what continues Moshe's work.

A *mitzvah* is not only its final act. The preparation, the effort, the approach, they are all part of it.
Rabbi Nachman taught that once beginnings flowed from *Pesach*; now they flow from *Purim.* In exile, *simchah* must reach the lowest places, because without it nothing stands.

From *Adar* we move to *Nissan.* Light rises from what lay below the line. What once was hidden becomes revealed. That is the opening *Adar* offers.

Rebbetzin Yehudis Golshevsky is the founder and director of Shiviti, an educational initiative based in Jerusalem. She teaches Chassidus, Jewish thought, and inner avodah to women worldwide, integrating classical Torah sources with lived spiritual awareness and depth.

🌐 **shiviti.org.il**
✉ **Info@shiviti.org.il**

ART "UNDERWATER"™ BY EVA BIBAS

Not the Plan – The Purpose: My Aliyah Story

BY LESLEY KAPLAN

WHERE IT ALL BEGAN

I was born and raised in Johannesburg, South Africa. Later I spent a year working in Cape Town, fulfilling my original dream of living by the sea.

Before *Aliyah*, I lived as a traditional Jew, surrounded by both Jewish and non-Jewish friends at a co-ed school. My family lit candles, said *kiddush* and *hamotzi* on Friday night, and gathered for *chagim*. We weren't great *shul* goers, but Judaism was present, warm, and familiar. As a teen, I started going to *shul* with friends and have childhood memories of *shul* around the *chagim*. Later, I was introduced more deeply to Judaism and to the idea of living in Israel through my husband-to-be.

My parents always followed what was happening in Israel through local news and Jewish newspapers. I had never been to Israel, and truthfully, it wasn't on the agenda. When I met my husband-to-be, he would only date women interested in making *Aliyah*. I joke now that I was either adventurous or stupid. I agreed to live here without ever seeing the country. My first visit was when we were engaged.

SAYING YES WITHOUT KNOWING

For me, *Aliyah* happened by default. I was a willing and able partner, but I didn't initiate it. Once the decision was made, we planned. We made *Aliyah* with our ten-month-old daughter, who is now almost 37. We were idealistic and thought we

PHOTO BY SARA DUNCAN

Hebrew, only a few words. We initially moved to an area with very few Anglos, which I wouldn't recommend today, but at the time it helped me learn the language and gain confidence.

I never would have dreamed that I'd be running a business, training and coaching clients, and negotiating with Israelis, all in Hebrew. It didn't happen at once. Over the years, it happened naturally, without me even realizing how far I'd come. Being open to change is essential for a successful *Aliyah*.

Not having close family here, our friends became our family. Through hard work, we built our first home in Maaleh Michmash in the Binyamin area, our first home in *Eretz Yisrael*. We felt a great sense of achievement.

In Israel, you feel and live Judaism, whether you're religious or not. The national holidays are the *chagim*. There's no need to ask for a day off for a chag. As a Jew, I feel safer here than anywhere else. I feel at home.

I believe strongly in a half-cup-full attitude. See the good, and the good will find you. See opportunities and greatness, and they will find you. Focus on what you can control, not what you can't. Every country has good and bad. Choosing to see the good here helps overcome the challenges.

would save money first. After two years, we decided to just do it, and we haven't looked back since. Planning is important, but it's also possible you'll never feel totally ready if you plan for too long. Every extra year waiting can mean losing opportunities that exist only once you are actually here.

My aspirations, though not yet defined goals, were clear. Building my life and career here. Building a family in the Jewish land. Finding the right community. Buying a home. These were dreams that became goals, and I'm proud to say we achieved them.

LEARNING LIFE FROM THE INSIDE

The beginning came with real challenges. Leaving family behind. Not knowing the language. When I arrived, I couldn't even speak a full sentence in

WORK, VOICE, AND STRENGTH

I made *Aliyah* in my 20s, which means most of my career has been built here. Before that, I was involved in consulting and leadership roles. Over the years, I naturally transitioned into areas that matter deeply to me: advancing others, entrepreneurship, collaboration, and personal and business growth.

I live by a simple rule: your word is your word. Honesty and ethics are the most important things to me. If I say I'll do something, I'll do it.

I was blessed with resilience and determination. When my mother died suddenly while I was 39 weeks pregnant, when I went through divorce, and when my son was critically ill in ICU for five weeks while I was also marrying off my daughter and completing my Masters, I didn't drop the ball. I showed up. Living here brought out a strength in me I didn't fully know I had: standing up for myself, being Jewish, standing up for my country, and finding my voice.

Women have an inner strength and quality unlike most men I know. Be proud of yourself and your strengths. Don't undermine what you're capable of. Believe in yourself, and do it.

WATER, PERSPECTIVE, AND PURIM

I'm a water baby. I love sea views. Caesaria's port has always been one of my favorite places. *BH*, I fulfilled a long-time dream—that became a goal—by moving to Netanya and seeing the sea every day. It calms me, even during busy times.

If you're struggling to make *Aliyah* or to start again, know that it's possible at any age. There will be challenges. Be patient. Follow your passion. Ask for help when needed.

Because this is shared around *Purim*, I think about *venahafoch hu*, moments when life turns upside down and leads to growth. She rose to the occasion and used her voice. Step beyond the safety of your comfort zone and trust your voice. Don't be afraid to be seen and heard.

When I look at my life today, I feel grateful that I chose Israel. My goal is to continue guiding and inspiring others, to be a positive role model for my children and grandchildren, and to keep building our wonderful country with purpose and gratitude.

Lesley Kaplan is a Business Strategy and Branding Coach, Organizational Consultant and Trainer, advancing businesses and nonprofits to success for 30+ years. Founder and host of the Monday Motivation 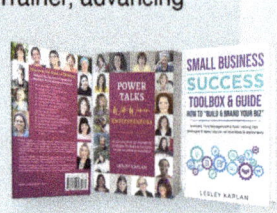 Spotlight Podcast, Israel Networking Hub, and social impact project ImpactIL™. Author of *Small Business Success Toolbox & Guide* and *Power Talks With Women Entrepreneurs*.

🌐 **lesleykaplan.com**
🌐 **impactil.org**

FINDING HOME IN EFRAT:
Space, Soul, and the People Who Show Up

BY MELISSA SUSSMAN

PHOTO BY BEN GOLDSTEIN / UNITYWARRIORS.ORG

When I first got married, my husband *David* and I lived in French Hill in Jerusalem. On paper, it made sense. It was affordable, close to the light rail, and in the holiest city in the world. It was a nice community, but it didn't feel like our community. It felt crowded, congested, and not very safe for kids. I also felt boxed in. I knew I wanted something else.

I was craving a small-town feel and real community, while still having access to a larger city. At the time, I wasn't sure that combination actually existed. Then we spent *Shabbat* in Efrat. I remember thinking, why am I on a hilltop in the middle of nowhere? I grew up on Long Island, about forty minutes outside New York City, surrounded by people and movement. This felt unfamiliar.

And then I met the people. That was it.

When we moved to Efrat in 2020, just a few months before COVID, the transition felt natural. Shortly after we arrived, a welcoming committee came to our door, not in a performative way, but in a "you matter" way. That moment set the tone for everything that followed.

THE FEEL OF EFRAT

Compared to Jerusalem, life in Efrat

feels more open-minded and grounded. There is physical, emotional, and spiritual space. The pace of life is slower, but not sleepy. People are busy raising families, working, learning Torah, volunteering, and showing up for one another without the constant pressure-cooker feeling.

The neighborhoods of Efrat are inspired by the seven species of Israel: *Te'ena, Rimon, Gefen, Tamar, Dagan, Zayit, and Dekel.*

Efrat has a beautiful Beit Midrash program, and my neighborhood, *Dagan*, offers weekly *shiurim*. Every neighborhood has its own vibrant learning scene. There are also many incredible shuls. If you're looking for a Carlebach-style davening, you can walk from *Dagan* to Rabbi Shlomo's shul in *Zayit*. I also love the English-speaking Chabad, which is warm, welcoming, and easy to connect with. Our family is part of *Reishit Dagancha*.

I'll admit, I'm often lazy on *Shabbat* and stay home with a book, but when I feel up for it, I head to *Reishit Dagancha*. Spiritual life here isn't forced; it's just present. Women are deeply involved in learning and communal life, which mattered a lot to me from the beginning. In my own neighborhood, there's even a book club for women, giving us a chance to connect, discuss, and learn together. The *shiurim* are thoughtful, inspiring, and grounding, giving many of us a renewed sense of purpose week after week.

I also participate in a weekly *Salatim Club*, where neighbors gather to sample and share our dips, a small, fun tradition

that fosters community and connection.

Despite how Efrat is sometimes labeled, the community is incredibly diverse. People come from all over the world. What unites them is belief in this land, in the Jewish people, and in building a meaningful life here.

WOMEN, WORK, AND SHOWING UP

Most women in Efrat work in remote jobs, healthcare, education, nonprofit work, and entrepreneurship. It is a working-mom community, and that reality is understood and respected. If you are juggling, help exists. Someone will pick up a child. Someone will step in. WhatsApp groups for jobs, carpools, favors, and recommendations genuinely support each other.

For Anglo women, building a career here is possible. It may require creativity, especially if you work primarily in English, but opportunities exist. Women actively support one another.

Motherhood in Efrat has a nostalgic quality. Kids walk to friends' houses, play outside, and disappear for hours on Shabbat afternoons. It feels reminiscent of how many of us grew up, with safety, independence, and trust.

Chesed is woven into daily life. Chasdei Efrat serves the community through food pantries, meal deliveries, wedding and bat mitzvah *gemachs*, medical equipment loans, support for families in mourning, and countless informal acts of kindness. When my husband's father passed away shortly after we moved, the community showed up consistently

and sincerely. That moment made me understand exactly where we were.

SCHOOLS AND EDUCATION

I have twin 11-year-olds, and like many Anglo parents, adjusting to the Israeli school system took time. Some things are less structured, some require advocacy, and flexibility is essential.

Efrat offers real choice. There is a wide religious spectrum, and parents select schools based on each child's needs. I send my children to two different schools, one more *Torani* and one *Mamlachti Dati*, both Anglo-friendly, both with smaller classes and personal attention. Many parents supplement with tutors or enrichment. Language support for *Olim* exists, and parental involvement is welcomed.

The community center offers excellent after-school activities, from music and dance to coding and sports. There is also an *Olim* Center that supports new families. Yes, bureaucracy exists. This is Israel. Patience helps, and sometimes chocolate.

HOUSING AND EVERYDAY LIFE

Housing in Efrat includes apartments, duplexes, cottages, and private homes across several neighborhoods. We started by renting, which gave us time to understand the community, and once we knew it was right, we bought.

Efrat is not inexpensive, but families often feel they get real value, with more space, greenery, walkability, and safety. Families tend to stay long-term and build roots. Daily life is active. You see people walking, running, biking, and spending time outdoors. There are parks, green spaces, and access to nature and history all around. Living in the Judean Hills grounds daily life in something older and deeper than modern routines.

FINAL THOUGHTS

The greatest gift of living in Efrat has been giving my children a childhood filled with independence, lifelong friendships, and the space to grow. My husband runs a tourism company, *David Sussman Israel Tours* and we often visit locations where Torah events actually took place,

PHOTO BY BEN GOLDSTEIN / UNITYWARRIORS.ORG

experiences that bring our learning and history vividly to life.

For me personally, the biggest adjustment has been navigating Israeli culture and living in Hebrew. It can be humbling and frustrating, but it's also part of the growth of truly building a life here.

There is a sense of belonging that is hard to explain. Not because it doesn't exist elsewhere, but because living here allows you to feel it more consistently, in small everyday moments. For Jewish women thinking about community, *Aliyah*, or belonging, I have learned this. Outside Israel, the focus often feels external. Inside Israel, it becomes internal. And in Efrat, there is room for the soul.

This article was contributed by the Sussman family.

Melissa Sussman is Head of Influencer Management and Brand Partnerships at *Barzel Media* and a longtime Israel advocate. She's also a personal stylist (**@melsfashionedit**). Melissa and her husband **David**, founder of *David Sussman Israel Tours*, live in Efrat with their twin son and daughter. Let's connect!

🌐 **barzelmedia.com**
✉ **Melissa@barzelmedia.com**
▣ **@melissa_ashley_sussman**

✉ **David@sussmanisraeltours.com**
▣ **@david_sussman_israel_tours**

SPONSORED

Aliyah was meant to be a dream
not a full-time job.

We help Olim navigate Israeli bureaucracy –
calmly, clearly, and professionally.

✓ Expert Legal & Medical Support

✓ Bituach Leumi & Kupat Cholim Advocacy

✓ Special-Needs Guidance & Coaching

WEiSLAW
Adv. Emanuel Weisgras Law Office
📞 +972 53-945-0487

Peace of Mind Starts Now
Book your free 30-minute consult.
weisgraslaw.com/tribe

Winter in Bloom:
Five Spectacular Wildflower Trails Across Israel

BY SUSANNAH SCHILD

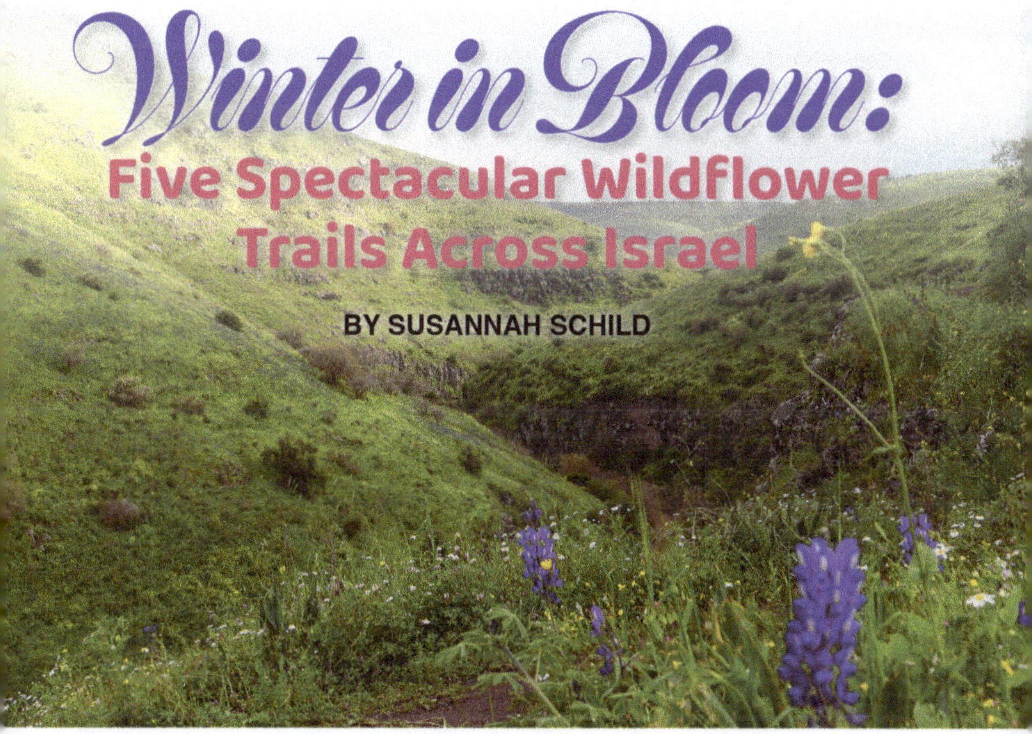

L ate winter is the time for cozying up indoors by the fireplace, away from the cold, rain, and snow… if you're in Europe or North America, that is. But in Israel? Winter is a peak flower season. Now is the best time to get outdoors, soak up some sun, and frolic in fields of colorful wildflowers. Birds are chirping, meadows are growing tall and green, and it feels like spring is already here.

There are plenty of flower-peeping trails around Israel. If you time it right, you'll find beautiful blooms in almost any natural space. But a few hiking trails stand out for dramatic scenery and sheer abundance of flowers. Imagine yourself prancing through fields of bouncing red anemones or gazing at a purple lupine-covered hilltop against a magical sunset. Bring along a picnic lunch and set yourself up for a feel-good, mid-winter outing in nature.

Here are five of the best flower trails in Israel you won't want to miss this season. Get out there and witness this wintertime wonder.

TEL SOCHO

(also known as Givat HaTurmosim)

Let's start with the basics. *Tel Socho*, otherwise known as *Givat HaTurmosim*, has become famous for its incredible lupine display in late winter. Tall purple flowers blanket the hillside in abundance, interspersed with the occasional red anemone or pink cyclamen.

PHOTOS BY SUSANNAH SCHILD

15

Although *Tel Socho* is best known for its flowers, there's plenty of history here too. *Socho* dates back to biblical times as part of the *Emek HaElah*, mentioned in the story of *David* and *Goliath*, where it served as a border town between Israelite and Philistine territory. At the back of the hill, ancient ruins await old olive presses, cisterns, and crumbling walls, the remnants of another era.

My family often makes a trip to *Givat HaTurmosim* near Beit Shemesh on *Shushan Purim*. Usually, this is the perfect time of year to catch the purple flowers in their full glory.

NAHAL TAVOR

Many people have never heard of *Nahal Tavor*, but it's hard to understand why. This is one of the most beautiful hikes in Israel, particularly during late winter.

At *Nahal Tavor*, an array of colorful flowers blossoms across rolling green hills, towering picturesquely above a gaping valley with a bubbling stream winding through. The scenery looks like something straight out of a Switzerland vacation brochure.

Aside from the wildflowers, there's also a beautiful waterfall—the Basalt Waterfall. It's a perfect spot for contemplating nature on cold or stormy days. On warmer days, you'll find hikers splashing in the cool water.

As if all this natural beauty weren't enough, *Nahal Tavor* was also the site of a great biblical battle between the Israelite and Canaanite armies. This is where Deborah and Barak fought Sisera, and the Canaanite chariots became stuck in the muddy stream on a miraculously stormy day.

Serious hikers can tackle the full 7.5-kilometer loop trail. Otherwise, enjoy a relaxed out-and-back stroll through wildflower-lined paths to the waterfall and back. Located in the Lower Galilee, *Nahal Tavor* is well worth the trip.

MINHAT MEGIDDO

Love beautiful wildflowers but can't handle a lengthy trek? *Minhat Megiddo* is the trail for you. This hidden gem in the Jezreel Valley sits right near *Tel Megiddo*, an ancient biblical city turned national park.

What makes *Minhat Megiddo* truly special are its multicolored anemones. In most places in Israel, these flowers appear in just one shade—crimson red. Here, however, you'll find fields of anemones in purple, pink, white, red, and every shade in between.

This short, easy trail is perfect for a photo-op. It's accessible, family-friendly, and delivers serious natural beauty. Combine the walk with a visit to nearby *Tel Megiddo* for a full day out.

DAROM ADOM

Perhaps the most quintessentially Israeli winter adventure is the flower-peeping festival in the south: *Darom Adom*. On the western side of Israel, between the Sharon Valley and the desert, several national parks and nature reserves explode with brilliant red anemones each February.

My favorite spot in the south is *Pura Nature Reserve*, where cheerful green meadows fill with bobbing blossoms, butterflies, and meandering paths as far as the eye can see.

Other popular locations include *Nahal Besor*, *Be'eri Forest*, and *Shokeda Forest*. With hiking and biking trails for every age and ability, this region offers something for everyone. Visiting the south is also a meaningful way to support communities deeply affected after October 7th.

ADULAM NATURE RESERVE

Adulam Nature Reserve wins the prize for ease and convenience. Located in the Judean Hills near Beit Shemesh, *Adulam* offers forests, hiking trails, Bar Kochba tunnels, ancient ruins—and plenty of flowers.

Almost any trail here bursts with winter wildflowers in February and March. Red anemones dominate the landscape, but you'll also spot calendula, wild mustard, and even wild asparagus in certain areas.

My favorite all-in-one route is the circular hike connecting the *Burgin* and *Itri* ruins. Along the way, you'll explore a remarkably preserved Second Temple-era city, complete with an ancient

synagogue, enjoy sweeping views along flower-lined paths, and visit a second ancient settlement.

There's something about the contrast between ancient stone ruins and cheerful red flowers under a bright winter sky that instantly lifts the spirit. *Adulam* is one of the best places near Jerusalem for greenery, history, and beauty on any winter day.

FLOWER FASCINATION

Israel may not boast snowcapped mountains or frozen lakes, but in late winter it offers something just as magical. Fields of wildflowers burst into color across the country, creating landscapes that rival even the Netherlands.

This season, don't wait indoors for spring to arrive. Take advantage of Israel's rich natural beauty, and chase away the winter blues with a visit to one of these stunning, flower-filled trails.

Susannah Schild is the creator of *Hiking the Holyland*, Israel's leading English language hiking resource, and author of *From Southerner to Settler: Unexpected Lessons from the Land of Israel*. She lives in Gush Etzion with her husband and six children.

🌐 hikingintheholyland.com
📷 @hikingtheholyland

AND WHAT WE'RE REALLY HUNGRY FOR

BY SHELLIE GRAFSTEIN

What Lives Beneath the Surface

Purim is a holiday of layers, much of it unseen. Emotional eating works the same way.

At its core, emotional eating is eating feelings that are too uncomfortable to feel. Sometimes it is eating for comfort, sometimes for protection, and sometimes to calm anxiety, soothe loneliness, or create a sense of stability when something inside feels shaky or unsafe. Food becomes a way to cope, a way to quiet what feels overwhelming, and a way to keep going when stopping to feel would feel like too much.

It's Not About Willpower

What emotional eating is not is a lack of discipline or willpower. This is where many women get stuck, believing they should be able to "do better" if they just tried harder. But emotional eating has nothing to do with trying harder. It has everything to do with how you learned to protect yourself.

Our bodies are wired first and foremost for survival. If food once helped you get through fear, stress, grief, or emotional pain, your body remembers that. It does not forget what worked. That is why emotional eating often feels automatic. The urge comes quickly, before you have time to think. You may not even feel hungry, yet the pull toward food feels urgent and familiar. The body reaches for what once brought relief.

What Food Is Really Standing In For

On the surface, it looks like food. Underneath, there is often fear, grief, disappointment, or longing that never had space to be felt. For many women, these emotions were set aside for years in order to function, raise families, and hold everything together. Food became something quiet and reliable, something that did not demand words.

Ta'anit Esther and the Willingness to Feel

This is also why Ta'anit Esther is so meaningful. Fasting is, in many ways, the opposite of emotional eating. Emotional eating says, "I can't feel this right now." Fasting says, "I am willing to sit with what comes up."

Esther fasted before she acted. She did not numb herself or distract herself. She created space to feel fear, vulnerability, and uncertainty, and through that space she connected to something deeper than herself.

This does not mean that fasting is about pushing ourselves or ignoring our bodies. Judaism has always been clear that we treat the body with care and respect. Still, there is something powerful about noticing what surfaces when we do not immediately soothe or distract. For many women, what comes up during a fast is not hunger for food at all, but hunger for calm, reassurance, safety, to feel held, and to be heard.

4 Ways to Make Ta'anit Esther More Meaningful (and Easier)

● **CONNECT TO THE MEANING OF THE FAST.**

Ta'anit Esther is not about food. It is about vulnerability, threat, and turning toward Hashem in a moment of danger. After the past three years, it is unfortunately very easy to connect to what it feels like to face an enemy who wants to annihilate us. Let the fast be rooted in meaning, not just hunger.

● **REMEMBER WHO IS LEADING.**

This mindset shift changed everything for me. I used to be a terrible faster. Once I truly understood that I was choosing the fast and that my body could follow my lead, it became much easier. There is something deeply empowering about realizing that discomfort does not get to run the show.

● **NOTICE WHAT YOUR BODY IS DOING FOR YOU.**

While you are fasting, your body is not busy digesting food. It is doing deep "housecleaning." Cells repair, systems reset, and the body gets a chance to do work it cannot usually do when it is constantly processing meals. Knowing this does not erase hunger, but it gives it meaning and context.

● **BREAK THE FAST WITH CARE.**

Begin with a large glass of water, warm or hot if possible (cold if you prefer). Pause for a few minutes and let your body register the hydration before moving on to food. It is a small act of kindness that makes a real difference.

Reframing Emotional Eating

This brings us to the deeper message. Emotional eating is not a failure. It is not a character flaw, and it is not something to be ashamed of. It is a coping strategy your body learned in order to keep you safe and help you survive.

When we understand that, everything changes. Instead of fighting ourselves, we become curious. Instead of judging, we listen. Instead of trying to control the behavior, we begin to understand the need underneath it. When the real need is acknowledged, the food slowly loses its purpose. Not overnight, and not through force, but through awareness and compassion.

Shellie Grafstein is a life coach and EFT practitioner helping women 60+ find calm, clarity, and freedom around emotional eating and life transitions. Her work focuses on understanding the root of eating patterns with compassion, not control.

✉ **grafsteinshellie@gmail.com**
📷 **grafsteinshellie**
🌐 **elevateshellie.com**

Hidden Guidance, Sudden Light

Purim reminds us that salvation can come in an instant, that even when things look stacked against us, *Hashem* is guiding events behind the scenes, and that what feels hidden, confusing, or painful can turn around in ways we could never imagine.

We are living through difficult days of fear, grief, and uncertainty, days when it can feel like darkness is winning. But the story of *Purim* teaches us otherwise. Light can break through suddenly. Redemption can arrive quietly. What looks impossible can change in the blink of an eye.

May this *Purim* bring healing, clarity, and comfort. May the hidden become revealed for the good, and may we merit to see light chase away darkness, in our lives and in the world, speedily and in our days.

———— SPONSORED ————

Energize Life Transformation

A 3-Month Holistic
Healing & Coaching Program

Heal your body, mind, and spirit —
and become a source of healing for your family.

Learn natural, Torah-aligned tools to
navigate physical pain, life challenges,
and relationship blocks
through energy healing and holistic guidance.

Malka Kornreich
Holistic Healing Coach &
Emotion Code Therapist

1.malkakornreich.com
office@malkakornreich.com

Begin your healing journey today.
Limited spaces available.

20

Herbal Self-Care, Inspired by Queen Esther

BY YAEL NEHAMA LOPEZ-RESPES

The holiday of *Purim* is one of, if not the most, feminine centered holidays in the Jewish calendar. Our beloved heroine, *Queen Esther*, is remembered for her extraordinary courage, humility, and unwavering faith under pressure.

Yet before she became the heroine of the *Purim* story, the *Megillah* offers us a quieter detail, one that speaks powerfully to women across generations:

"וּבְהַגִּיעַ תֹּר נַעֲרָה...שִׁשָּׁה חֳדָשִׁים בְּשֶׁמֶן הַמֹּר"
Six months with oil of myrrh.
—*Esther* 2:12

Esther's rise in the Persian court did not begin with a crown or a decree. It began with preparation. Slow, intentional, embodied preparation. When read through both *Torah* and historical context, her beauty rituals reveal a sacred model of feminine self-care rooted in patience, refinement, and spiritual readiness.

Esther's Beauty Rituals, Text, Tradition, and History

Across ancient cultures, herbs were understood as bridges between body, emotion, and spirit. They were used not only for adornment, but for balance and preparation. The *Megillah* describes two distinct stages of preparation:

Six months with oil of myrrh, שֶׁמֶן הַמֹּר

Six months with perfumes and cosmetics, בְּשָׂמִים וּבְתַמְרוּקֵי נָשִׁים

Myrrh, *mor*, is a resin derived from the Commiphora tree and was among the most valued botanicals in the ancient world. Persian, Egyptian, and Indian sources describe myrrh oil as antiseptic, anti-inflammatory, and deeply nourishing to the skin. It was often used to heal, soften, and restore after prolonged exposure to stress or harsh environments.[1]

Chazal note that myrrh was not merely cosmetic, but purifying. The *Malbim* explains that the extended preparation refined both body and disposition, cultivating inner composure alongside outer grace.[2]

The second phase likely involved *besamim*, fragrant botanicals and herbal cosmetics common in royal courts, including frankincense for its calming and spiritually elevating qualities, rose for hydration and its association with dignity and royalty, saffron for its brightening and mood lifting properties, and aloe for its cooling and restorative effects.

2 Feminine Preparation as Spiritual *Avodah*

Esther's preparation lasted a full year. This was not considered indulgence. It was a slow and meaningful initiation into her future role.

Judaism does not separate body and soul. The body is viewed as a *kli*, a vessel for holiness. Caring for it gently and intentionally is a form of *avodah*, self care in the truest sense, especially for women whose lives often revolve around giving, holding, and enduring.

The *Rambam* teaches that emotional equilibrium is essential for wisdom and clarity.[3] Modern science echoes this understanding. Slow, sensory rituals calm the nervous system, regulate stress hormones, and support emotional resilience.

Queen Esther models a feminine path of transformation, quiet strength rooted in grounded presence and trust in the unfolding of time. Through herbal self-care, we follow this same path. Herbs become a language of *emuna*, partnering with *Hashem* through the natural wisdom embedded in creation.

3 Simple Herbal Rituals for Today's Jewish Woman

A Calming *Adar Purim* Bath

As joy increases in *Adar*, grounding becomes essential.

Blend one cup Dead Sea or Epsom salt, half a cup dried rose petals, a quarter cup chamomile, and one tablespoon lavender buds.

Soak for fifteen to twenty minutes, breathing slowly.

Rose supports emotional balance, chamomile calms the nervous system, and lavender reduces tension, allowing joy to remain expansive rather than overwhelming.[4]

Gentle Facial Steam

A ritual of renewal and clarity.

Use rose petals, calendula, and chamomile. Place two tablespoons of each in a clean pot with hot water. Add several drops of lavender oil if not sensitive. Steam gently for five to seven minutes.

This ritual improves circulation, softens skin, opens pores, and invites mindful presence.

DIY Herbal Oil Infusion Inspired by *Shemen HaMor*

Fill a jar with dried calendula, rose, or lavender. Cover completely with olive or almond oil. Infuse in a dark place for four to six weeks, shaking daily, or gently warm for quicker use.

Apply after bathing.

Calendula supports skin repair, rose nourishes and uplifts, and olive oil deeply moisturizes, echoing ancient practices still validated today.[5]

Herbs Supporting Women's Wellbeing

- **Rose** supports emotional balance and skin hydration.
- **Lavender** supports stress relief and sleep.
- **Chamomile** is calming and anti-inflammatory.
- **Calendula** supports skin healing and lymphatic flow.
- **Rosemary** supports circulation and mental clarity.
- **Sage** supports grounding and hormonal balance.

4 *Purim*, Revealing Hidden Radiance

Purim is the *chag* of *hester*, concealment giving way to revelation. Herbal practices work in much the same way. Quietly and gradually, beneath the surface. With continued use, inner radiance emerges. Not instant beauty, but one deeply rooted in the sacred art of self care.

Queen Esther's beauty was modest, dignified, and aligned. Through simple and natural self-care, we enter *Purim*

regulated rather than depleted, joyful rather than scattered. Ready to celebrate, to give, and to be seen in our truest light.

May you be blessed to recognize your deep worth, to reveal your inner beauty, and to see yourself as the queen you already are. Most importantly, may you care for yourself with the love you deserve. *Chag Purim Sameach.*

Yael Nehama Lopez-Respes is an educator, writer, fiber artist and folk herbalist who enjoys exploring the meeting place of Torah, feminine spirituality, and herbal traditions. A creative at heart, she enjoys writing about the sacred mundane, embodied Judaism and practice, along with spending time with her adult children and sweet grandchildren.

✉ **yael.nehama@gmail.com**
📷 **@Village_wisewoman**

Sources

Manniche, L. *An Ancient Egyptian Herbal*. University of Texas Press.

Malbim on *Esther* 2:12.

Rambam, Hilchot De'ot 3:1.

Herz, R. The Emotional, Cognitive, and Biological Basics of Olfaction. *Chemical Senses*.

Chevallier, A. *Encyclopedia of Herbal Medicine*. DK Publishing.

The Rhythm Within

UNDERSTANDING A **WOMAN'S HORMONAL JOURNEY,** FROM FIRST CYCLE TO FULL CIRCLE

WITH DR. ELISSA HELLMAN, MD, FACOG

A woman's hormonal story is not a single chapter. It is a lifelong rhythm, unfolding quietly, steadily, and often misunderstood. From puberty to pregnancy, from postpartum to perimenopause, our hormones are not something to fix, but something to understand, respect, and live alongside.

At its core, a woman's hormonal system operates on two intertwined rhythms. There is the long arc of life, puberty, reproductive years, and menopause, and there is the shorter monthly rhythm, the menstrual cycle, with its natural fluctuations in energy, mood, and focus. Both are normal. Both are purposeful. And neither is a mistake.

One of the most empowering truths a woman can hear is this: what your body is doing is usually exactly what it is meant to do.

Normal Is Not a Problem

In recent years, conversations about hormones have become louder, and sometimes heavier. We hear messages about balancing, optimizing, or working with our cycles, often delivered with strict rules and constant monitoring. While awareness can be helpful, over medicalizing normal female biology can quietly create anxiety.

Many women begin to feel pressure to do everything right. Eat the right foods on the right cycle day. Exercise according to a precise hormonal schedule. Take the correct supplements. Never miss a step. But this constant vigilance can disconnect women from their bodies rather than attune them.

Understanding your cycle does not mean controlling it. It means noticing patterns with curiosity, not judgment. You might realize that at certain points in the month you feel more social, while at others you need rest. That awareness allows for self compassion, not perfection.

Hormones and the Whole Woman

Hormones are not limited to reproduction. They are chemical messengers that affect the entire body, including the brain. Estrogen and progesterone receptors exist throughout the nervous system, which is why hormonal shifts influence not only physical health,

but also energy, clarity, emotions, and thought patterns.

This is why major life transitions, puberty, pregnancy, postpartum, and menopause, bring changes that are both physical and emotional. It is not weakness. It is biology.

Lifestyle factors such as sleep, movement, nourishment, and emotional load also play a role. Not because they must be perfectly aligned to your cycle, but because basic care matters at every stage of life. The body does not require micromanagement. It requires consistency, rest, and respect.

Some women find it helpful to keep a simple journal for a few months, noting how they feel at different times in their cycle. Not to analyze endlessly, but to recognize personal rhythms. Knowledge becomes empowering when it reduces confusion, not when it creates pressure.

Fertility, Timing, and Sensitivity

Because this conversation spans generations, fertility must be approached with care. Not every woman is trying to conceive. Not every woman can. And not every woman's journey unfolds according to plan.

Hormones do not change because a woman is focused on her career or building a life. They follow biological timelines, not personal ambition. However, fertility does naturally decline with age. This reality deserves honesty without fear.

For women over forty who hope to conceive, early conversations with a physician can be valuable. Not as a declaration of urgency, but as information. The goal is not to rush or alarm, but to avoid losing time unintentionally if assistance is needed.

At the same time, it is essential to hold space for what is outside of control. Fertility journeys are deeply personal, and no one path defines a woman's worth.

Pregnancy, Postpartum, and the Hormonal Drop

Pregnancy is marked by a dramatic rise in hormone levels. These shifts support the body's extraordinary work, and they can also heighten emotions and physical changes. When pregnancies occur close together, the body has biologically returned to ovulation, even if emotionally or physically it still feels tender.

Postpartum, however, brings one of the most abrupt hormonal changes a woman experiences. Hormone levels drop quickly after delivery, creating a state often compared to a sudden mini menopause. This rapid shift can affect mood, energy, and mental health.

This is why postpartum depression and anxiety are not failures. They are signals. Signs include persistent sadness, anxiety, emotional numbness, or feeling disconnected from oneself. Support begins with awareness, rest, honest conversations, and involving both medical professionals and loved ones.

The bounce back culture does women a disservice. Healing is not linear, and rest is not optional. It is necessary.

Menopause: An Ending and a Becoming

Menopause is defined as twelve consecutive months without a period. The years leading up to it, known as perimenopause, vary widely in length and experience. Some women feel very little. Others feel profound shifts, physically, mentally, and emotionally.

What is often overlooked is the mental and emotional transition. As hormone production gradually declines, the brain adapts. Thought patterns shift. Memory, focus, and mood can change. This is not a flaw. It is a rewiring.

Just as a girl becomes a different person between ages five and fifteen, a woman evolves again in midlife. While symptoms can be challenging, this stage can also be deeply grounding.

Many women describe feeling more settled, more confident, and more themselves. With children often older and life more stable, menopause can mark a powerful return to inner clarity, especially when symptoms are addressed with appropriate medical care and emotional support.

Across Generations: Less Fixing, More Support

Perhaps the most important message across all stages is this: comparison helps no one.

Even though women share the same biological framework, the way hormones are experienced is deeply personal. Perimenopause and menopause, in particular, can bring significant mental and emotional shifts. Mood changes, fogginess, irritability, or feeling unlike oneself are real parts of this transition, and they are not always something a woman can control.

This is not about attitude or effort. Menopause is not something that can be fixed by simply getting into a better mood or taking off a sweater and expecting everything to feel fine. A woman's body is going through real changes, and she is the one living inside them.

When we compare our experiences or direct others based on what worked for us, it often does more harm than good. It makes women second guess themselves, doubt their instincts, and look for answers in places that may not be reliable or supportive. Instead of feeling understood, they are left wondering if something is wrong with them.

Support looks different. It is not about telling someone what she should do

because of your own experience. It is about meeting her where she is. If a woman is having a really hard time with her baby, support does not sound like, "When I had my kids, they were all sleep trained by four weeks." It sounds like, "This looks really hard. How can I help?" Sometimes that help is as simple and meaningful as offering to watch the baby so she can take a nap.

When support replaces comparison, women feel less alone. They feel trusted in their own experience and less pressured to measure themselves against someone else's story. And that kind of understanding creates space for real connection, across stages, across generations, and across very different hormonal journeys.

Dr. Elissa Hellman, MD, FACOG is an OBGYN in Israel with two decades of clinical experience. She also runs a telehealth gynecology practice focused on the health needs of Jewish women. She offers one on one virtual consultations to address gaps in education Jewish women face throughout their reproductive years.

🌐 drelissahellmanmd.com
✉ info@drelissahellmanmd.com

Removing the Mask:

Purim, Style, and the Power of Your True Self

BY DEVORA GOLAN

What Purim Reveals

Purim has always been one of my favorite holidays. It's the day that invites us to dress up, and to play with identity and self expression. As a personal stylist who has helped hundreds of women bring out their true selves through style, I have seen firsthand how clothing can be a powerful tool to amplify confidence, communicate inner strength, and help a woman step fully into her power.

Style becomes a declaration:
This is me. I deserve to be seen.

There is a lesson in *Purim* that resonates deeply here. Beneath the costumes lies a message about revealing who we truly are. The story itself, how *Esther* moves from hiding her identity to courageously revealing it in order to save her people, reflects real transformation. Style can do the same. When chosen with intention, clothing becomes a reflection of who you truly are, not a cover for who you think you should be.

Your clothes are so much more than fabric. They are a signal to yourself and to the world of who you are. Choosing clothing that feels aligned with your personality and your mood can instantly elevate your energy. A small shift, deciding to wear something bold, structured, or vibrant instead of your go-to comfortable but boring ensemble, can change the tone of your entire day.

Dressing with Intention

Imagine putting on a top in your favorite color that turns your same old routine into a moment of celebration. Or walking into a meeting wearing that pair of shoes that makes you feel unstoppable. These are not superficial choices; they are declarations. This is me. I am capable. I deserve to be seen. When practiced daily, style becomes an act of personal empowerment. It is permission to have fun, to express yourself, and to celebrate your uniqueness without hesitation. The best part is that you don't need anyone else's approval to feel this power. It is yours to claim.

Esther's story is the ultimate guide to presence and inner strength. Even when it was difficult, she stepped up to the challenge. She did what she had to do and showed up with clarity, grace, and conviction. Personal style works in much the same way. The way you dress can help you approach every situation with confidence and purpose. A structured blazer signals authority and readiness. A vibrant dress communicates energy and optimism.

A monochrome look conveys sophistication and control. Each choice becomes a tool to help you embody the qualities you want to project.

Stepping into your power is deeply personal and can mean something different to everyone. Sometimes it is commanding the attention of a room filled with people. Other times it is simply the ease of showing up as your true self with friends and family. Power often shows up as magnetism. Style is one of the most immediate ways to embody it. Think about the mornings when you feel a little off or unsure. An outfit that makes you feel good can instantly shift your mood and the way you carry yourself.

Style can also give you the courage to take bold steps. Wearing a color that makes you feel alive might be the push you need to speak up in a meeting. Choosing a structured outfit can help you feel more grounded when presenting your ideas. Even something as small as a signature accessory you love, a necklace, bracelet, or ring, can become a talisman of confidence, reminding you of your capabilities as you move through the day.

Not Just for Special Occasions

The most effective way to find the style that reflects your highest self is through experimentation and awareness. There is no right answer for everyone. Step outside your comfort zone and try something you would not normally reach for. You do not need to buy a whole new wardrobe to do this. Look into your existing closet and pair pieces together in ways you would not usually consider. Play with color and contrast, and notice what makes you feel stronger and more confident.

Your Style, Your Crown
Think of your wardrobe as a toolkit.

You also do not have to wait for *Purim* or a special occasion to harness this power. A sequin skirt does not need to be saved for an event. Try pairing it with a t-shirt or a crisp white button-down for an everyday look that carries creativity and joy. If a big change feels intimidating, even a subtle shift can have a profound impact. This is not about following trends or impressing others. It is about aligning your outer expression with your inner energy so that every choice feels intentional.

Each outfit is a way to articulate your personality and highlight your unique qualities. Every day, you have the opportunity to step out of old patterns and into a more elevated version of yourself. Style is not about perfection.

It is about presence, self-expression, and embodying your feminine power. Clothing becomes a vehicle to remove layers of uncertainty and disguise, revealing the confident, joyful woman beneath.

This *Purim*, and every day beyond, consider this: What mask am I ready to let go of? What version of myself do I want to show the world? Which pieces in my wardrobe help me embody that energy?

Step into it. Celebrate it. Your style is your crown. Wear it like the queen you are!

Devora Golan is a Transformational Stylist who helps women create impact though Intentional Style. Through her signature *STAR* method she guides clients to curate Power Outfits and cultivate the Mindset that activates their inner magic and lets their radiant personalities shine. She loves helping women discover how personal style can unlock newfound confidence and open doors to extraordinary possibilities.

 @devoragolan
 devoragolan@gmail.com

THE MARATHON OF LIFE:

WELLNESS, DISCIPLINE & EMUNA

WITH BEATIE DEUTSCH

BY NAOMI JOURNO

Some interviews don't feel like interviews at all. They feel like sitting down with a best friend who reminds you of your own strength. Speaking with Beatie Deutsch was exactly that. An extraordinary powerhouse, Beatie is the Israeli national champion in the marathon and half marathon, a speaker, and a devoted mother. Her journey is a powerful blend of *emuna*, dedication, motherhood, and unexpected transformation. As you read, you may find yourself inspired to trust the process, show up anyway, and take that first step forward to work out, even on the days you don't feel like it.

PHOTO BY SARA DUNCAN

WHAT'S ONE PART OF YOUR JOURNEY THAT MOST PEOPLE DON'T KNOW BUT SHAPED WHO YOU ARE AS AN ATHLETE AND AS A JEWISH WOMAN?

I grew up very religious. I went to one of the most Orthodox girls' seminaries in Jerusalem, and I started off my married life with my husband learning in *kollel*.

What I've learned about my own religious journey is that you're constantly evolving in your relationship with *Hashem*. Even though it sometimes feels like Judaism is defined by external behavior, and people make judgments about where you're holding religiously based on what they see, it's really so much more about your internal connection with *Hashem*.

Judaism is deeply about our thoughts, intentions, and feelings. I think people forget that and focus too much on what you're doing and how you look.

HOW DID YOU START RUNNING SERIOUSLY, AND WHEN DID YOU REALIZE YOU HAD REAL POTENTIAL?

I started running after giving birth to to my fourth child in 2016. I hadn't exercised in six years, and I wanted to get back in shape. I needed a goal on the calendar to motivate me, so I signed up for a marathon knowing absolutely nothing and just jumped right in.

I had an amazing first marathon experience and time, but I didn't realize my potential at the beginning. People think that from the start I knew I was good, but I really didn't.

Less than three years later, in 2019, I won my first national championship. I ran a 2:42 marathon, and that's when I realized I had serious potential.

HOW DO YOU STAY CONSISTENT WITH TRAINING WHILE BEING A VERY BUSY JEWISH MOM WITH A FULL LIFE?

I stay consistent because my goals genuinely excite me, and I know I can't reach them without showing up. Once I get my training done, it's off my mind and I can move on with my day. I see consistency as my responsibility, doing my part and then trusting *Hashem* with the results. I also love how running makes me feel, and I'm grateful that I get to do it.

WHAT EXCITES YOU MOST ABOUT CHASING YOUR OLYMPIC DREAM?

I'm curious about my potential. We often get locked into where we are right now, and things that feel far away seem impossible. I constantly remind myself that I have no idea what could be in store for me.

There are so many doors waiting to be opened. I love living my life with excitement about the future and not knowing what's coming next.

WHAT'S ONE THING WOMEN OFTEN OVERLOOK WHEN CARING FOR THEIR BODIES?

Exercise actually creates energy. When you feel tired, movement is often exactly what you need. Even a short workout releases endorphins, lifts your mood, and leaves you feeling more alive. Don't listen to the voice that says you're too tired, just start.

WHEN EVERYTHING SAYS "NOT TODAY," HOW DO YOU PUSH THROUGH AND SHOW UP ANYWAY?

I remind myself that the tired voice isn't who I am. It's just my brain seeking comfort. I choose to listen to my *neshama*, the part that wants growth. I keep it simple. I tell myself I'm only going out for five minutes. Once I start, I usually keep going. You have to be your own biggest cheerleader.

WHEN YOU'RE STANDING AT THE STARTING LINE OF A MAJOR RACE, WHAT GOES THROUGH YOUR MIND?

I don't show up expecting miracles, but I know that every single step of the way is a miracle.

By the time you reach the starting line, you've already done all the hard work. Now the rest is in *Hashem*'s hands. We don't control the outcome. We only control our effort.

I always say a paragraph of *Tehillim* and remind myself that *Hashem* is in control and that my strength comes from Him. The starting line is the beginning of a celebration.

WHEN YOUR BODY HURTS, HOW DO YOU DEAL WITH PHYSICAL PAIN?

There are two types of pain. There is good pain, the pain that comes from pushing yourself in a race, and then there

is bad pain, which usually means injury.

I used to push through everything, but I've learned to listen to my body. Sometimes it's an imbalance. Sometimes it's a muscle issue. Sometimes it's a bone, and you really do need rest.

If I can't run, I cross train with swimming or cycling. Injuries teach gratitude. So many parts of our body work together every single day without us noticing.

It reminds me of *Asher Yatzar*. If one small opening doesn't function properly, the whole system fails. Running is the same. When you're injured, you realize what a gift your body is.

HOW DO YOU BALANCE AMBITION WITH ACCEPTING YOUR LIMITS?

I believe in having big desires, but also in understanding that I don't control the outcome.

I'm ambitious, and ambition is important. But you can't rely on achievements to feel whole. You have to fully love who you are, separate from what you accomplish. You are not your achievements.

I believe you only reach your potential once you become complete before achieving it. That takes growth and openness. And every time I think I'm there, there's always more work to do.

For me, the recurring theme is surrendering control. *Hashem* is in the driver's seat. We choose our attitude, our response, and our perspective.

CAN YOU SHARE A MOMENT WHERE YOU CLEARLY FELT HASHEM GUIDING YOU?

I ran the Berlin Marathon this past September. It was my first race back after two and a half years of injury. I ran a 2:40 marathon and hoped it would qualify me for the European Championships.

I was told I could be on the team, but the marathon was scheduled for Shabbat. I accepted it and moved on.

About a month later, my coach messaged me and said they moved the marathon to Sunday and I could be on the Israeli team. I hadn't campaigned or pushed for it. I believe *Hashem* wanted me there.

That moment felt like a hug from *Hashem*, like He was saying, "I see your faith, and I'm making this possible."

WHAT'S YOUR BEST TIP FOR BEGINNERS WHO WANT TO START RUNNING?

It takes about 30 days to integrate a new habit. In the beginning, it won't feel easy, and that's normal. But if you stay consistent, you'll reach a point where you're pleasantly surprised by how much you enjoy it and how good it feels.

Don't expect it to feel natural right away. Give yourself time. Showing up regularly is what creates the shift.

WHAT SHOULD MORE ADVANCED RUNNERS FOCUS ON TO LEVEL UP?

Intervals.

Don't always run at the same pace. If you want to get stronger and faster, you need to include workouts where you run hard for a period of time, followed by rest, and then repeat.

High intensity interval training is key for improving speed. You can start with something simple, like six repetitions of 400 meters, and build from there.

WHAT MESSAGE FROM THE MEGILLAH DOES THE WORLD NEED TODAY?

Unity.

Haman said we were scattered and divided. When Jews love, respect, and accept one another, even while serving *Hashem* differently, we are strong.

Beatie Deutsch is the Israeli national champion in the marathon and half marathon. A mother of five, she applies the discipline of elite athletic training to the real marathon of life. After taking up running later in life, she turned professional, pursuing Olympic qualification and inspiring women around the world to dream big, stay committed, and keep moving forward.

🌐 beatiedeutsch.com
✉ beatiedeutsch@gmail.com

5 Ways to Build a Relationship Fit for a King and Queen

BY DANIELLA RUDOFF

Purim is all about masks. And when it comes to dating, that's really the question people are asking: how do you know when someone is showing who they really are or if they are putting on a dating version of themselves just to make a good impression? This could be related to knowing to go on another date or if the person is a good person to marry.

There are no rules that fit every situation. Dating is not one- size- fits- all. Every individual is different. But there are things you can pay attention to that help you understand what is real and what is not.

1 NOTICE PRESENCE, NOT PERFORMANCE

One of the first things I pay attention to is eye contact.

If a person can enjoy a conversation and really be "present", if they are 'with you' and not distracted or looking around for the next thing to entertain them, that tells you something about their true interest in you.

If someone is always looking elsewhere during the conversation, always distracted, always searching for something else, that is something to notice.

There are people who are very good actors. They are charming, sociable, and know how to make it seem like they are interested.

Presence is different. Presence shows who someone really is.

2 WATCH CONSISTENCY AND MOMENTUM AFTER THE DATE

What happens after the date matters just as much as what happens during the date.

Consistency is one of the clearest indicators of character. Are they caring afterward? Are they interested? Do they follow through?

Momentum matters, especially in the beginning, as you are getting to know each other. In my experience, seeing each other every two to four days is very natural. When there is too much time in between dates, people start questioning and don't allow a relationship to develop. Once questioning starts, it creates a crack in the foundation of the potential relationship.

If you're really interested in the person you are dating, then try to meet every two to four days. I know you are each busy, but try to make the time.

I don't believe in playing "hard to get". Showing interest builds relationships. Interest creates safety, and safety allows something to grow.

3 PAY ATTENTION TO BALANCE AND REAL INTEREST

A relationship is not "give and take". It is important for each person in the couple to focus on what I can give. If each person in the couple "gives", then each person "receives".

Pay attention to whether there is real interest. Do they want to know about your family, your work, your education, and your hobbies? If you share something important, do they remember it later?

Balance does not mean asking questions back and forth like an interview. It means the conversation flows naturally, with curiosity and care on both sides.

When one person carries the entire conversation, that is something to notice.

4 RESPECT CLOSURE AS PART OF DIGNITY

Closure is extremely important.

Leaving people hanging is agonizing. If someone does not want to continue, it is important to close it clearly and respectfully.

If you are unsure, going on a second date can help clarify. But if you know you do not want to go out again, then don't.

Don't ghost anyone. Say thank you and tell them: "It was so nice meeting you, but I don't think it's a good fit to go out on another date". This allows both people to move forward.

Closing one door allows another door to open. Closure is not rejection. It is dignity.

5 BUILD THE RELATIONSHIP THROUGH GIVING AND ROYALTY

Many women want to feel cared for. Many men want to give, but sometimes they are afraid because of mixed messages in the world.

Giving is not about who is better. It is about developing and nurturing a relationship.

On *Purim*, we talk about giving, but not in a way that makes someone feel like an *evyon*, a poor person. We want to feel like a Queen , like *Esther HaMalka*.

A healthy, happy relationship can appear like a King and a Queen. Not because one is above the other, but because they honor each other. When a King gives to his Queen, he crowns her. When a Queen gives to her King, she crowns him.

They are constantly building each other up from their deepest interest to make their spouse feel special; creating dignity, warmth, and emotional safety.

SETTING THE TONE FROM THE VERY BEGINNING

This positive, giving approach starts even before the first date. It starts with the phone call.

If you smile when you speak, it changes the tone of your voice. "Hi, how are you?" sounds very different when it is said with warmth and a smile. Positive energy creates and attracts positive energy.

From this point, a giving, positive foundation begins forming. Maybe it will continue. Maybe it won't. Either way, you have practiced the muscle of successfully connecting to someone. You have created a respectful interaction in the world.

Your positive connecting muscles will be stronger and will serve you well when you meet your spouse.

LEARNING THE SKILLS AND STAYING OPEN

Not everyone comes into dating knowing how to communicate naturally. Some people care deeply, but they are nervous. They don't know how to express interest or how to have a balanced conversation. That does not mean they are not sincere.

These are skills that can be learned. Communication, presence, and emotional balance are soft skills, and they matter just as much as formal education or a high level profession. Relationships require learning how to interact, how to listen, and how to show care in a healthy way.

Staying open is also essential. Very rigid expectations can close doors that *Hashem* may want to open. When we are open, realistic, and willing to grow, we allow the right connection to unfold in its time.

AT EVERY STAGE OF LIFE

This applies in your twenties, thirties, forties, and beyond.

It is important to know yourself, but also to be realistic. It is also important to learn to step out of your comfort zone like *Queen Esther* did.

Just remember that very rigid "lists" can close doors that *Hashem* may want to open.

Ultimately, *Hashem* is in charge.

That is also the message of *Purim*: behind the masks, *Hashem* is guiding everything quietly and precisely, even when we don't see it yet.

May we each be able to bring the *geula* for *Am Yisrael* completely by creating happy Jewish couples.

Daniella Rudoff is a Global Jewish Matchmaker, Dating consultant, and Marriage educator known as *The Marriage Architect*, guiding singles toward meaningful, lasting relationships and happy, successful marriages. She teaches communication and relationship building skills, personally mentors clients, and builds connections with depth and integrity. Daniella lives in Israel and works with singles worldwide.

🌐 MarriageArchitect.com
✉ MarriageArchitect@gmail.com

The Home as a Training Ground

What Bullying, Siblings, and School Teach Us About Emotional Responsibility

BY RIVKA FISHMAN

Most parents wish they could shield their children from pain. From exclusion. From the unkind words that linger long after the school day ends. Many begin parenting hoping their child will never experience bullying at all.

But the reality is different.

Children cannot control how others behave. They can only learn how to respond. And they cannot learn that alone.

One of the most important messages for parents, teachers, and school administrators to understand is that emotional strength does not develop by accident. It is taught, modeled, and practiced over time. Children need adults beside them—not to rescue them from every discomfort, but to guide them as they learn how to handle it.

Support Without Rescue

When adults witness a child being treated unkindly, the instinct is often to step in immediately and fix it. But there is a critical difference between rescuing and supporting.

Rescuing looks like swooping in, highlighting the hurt, confronting other children, and unintentionally

escalating the situation. Supporting looks quieter. It looks like presence. It means noticing what is happening, correcting unacceptable behavior, and calmly teaching the group what is and is not acceptable.

In schools, teachers are responsible for creating environments where children feel safe, secure, and watched over. When adults intervene calmly and without drama, children learn that boundaries exist and that their emotional needs matter.

At the same time, children must also learn that they are responsible for how they handle what comes their way. These two truths must exist together.

The Invisible Bucket

One effective way to teach emotional responsibility is through the idea of the invisible bucket. Every person carries an unseen bucket that holds their thoughts and feelings about themselves and the world.

When the bucket is full, we feel calm and happy. When it is empty, we feel sad, angry, or lonely.

Children can be taught that when someone is being mean, it is often because that person's bucket is empty. They may try to fill it by dipping into someone else's bucket. Understanding this helps children realize that bullying is not about them.

It may still feel painful or annoying. But when a child understands that there is nothing wrong with them, the experience does not become an identity they carry into adulthood.

Coaching Children Through Bullying

When a child is being bullied, parents take on the role of coach. The first step is empathy. A child needs to feel heard and understood before anything else.

The next step is teaching tools.

One powerful tool is learning to respond calmly, without showing how hurt they feel. Children can be taught to respond as if the comment did not bother them. This does not mean it did not hurt. It means they do not give the other child the satisfaction of knowing they caused pain.

This takes practice, role-playing, and patience. It is not easy, but it is effective and worth the effort.

Parents should not rescue their children from every uncomfortable moment. Instead, they can communicate belief in their child's ability to handle the situation, while remaining present to guide and support them through it.

Responding calmly helps prevent projecting past pain onto a child's present experience.

When Your Child Is Hurting Others

Learning that your child is bullying someone else can be deeply unsettling. The first response should be curiosity, not anger.

Parents need to understand what is happening and why, without excusing the behavior. Bullying is never acceptable. It does not matter if a child is competitive, impulsive, frustrated, or overwhelmed. Being mean, rude, or unkind is not allowed.

Every situation is different. Some children need help building confidence. Others need support with impulse control or managing frustration. Whatever the cause, it must be addressed consistently and seriously.

This is also a teaching moment. Children learn that feelings are valid, but behavior has limits.

Siblings and the Home Environment

The home is often the hardest place to manage these dynamics, and also the most important.

Not all sibling conflict is bullying. Some disagreements are mutual and temporary. But when one child consistently targets another, parents must step in.

Clear rules matter. We do not call each other names. We do not hit. We do not

When a Parent's Own Past Is Triggered

Bullying often brings up something deeper for parents.

There is a statistic that approximately 80 percent of children who are bullied have a parent who was bullied themselves. This is likely not because being a victim is genetic. It is because unresolved childhood pain can make even small situations feel overwhelming.

A parent who was bullied naturally does not want their child to go through what they went through. That reaction is human. But reacting too quickly can unintentionally turn the child into a victim rather than a child dealing with someone else's unkind behavior.

Parents benefit from recognizing their triggers. Trauma therapy can be helpful, especially when memories still cause physical reactions in the body. When therapy is not accessible, awareness becomes essential.

Parents can pause, breathe, and say, "That must not have felt nice. I want to help you. Let me think about the best next step."

put each other down. These boundaries must be enforced every time.

Children also need positive attention so that misbehavior does not become the only way they feel seen. The home is the first place children learn how to treat others.

Regulation Starts With the Parent

Children learn emotional regulation from regulated adults.

Taking one minute to breathe before pickup, before walking into the house, or before responding to a difficult moment can change everything. Starting from a calm place allows parents to respond thoughtfully instead of reacting from anxiety.

Small moments, practiced consistently, build emotional strength over time.

This Is a Process

This work is not quick, and it is not perfect. It unfolds slowly, in ordinary moments, in after-school conversations, sibling disagreements, quiet pauses before reacting. Parents will get it right some days and miss the mark on others. That, too, is part of the learning.

Children do not need flawless parents. They need present ones. Adults who stay beside them, who believe in their strength even when they are struggling, and who show them, again and again, that difficult emotions can be handled without falling apart.

When children grow up in environments where feelings are acknowledged,

boundaries are clear, and adults remain calm and steady, they internalize something lasting: that other people's behavior does not define them. That discomfort can be tolerated. That they are capable.

Over time, these lessons take root. They become resilience. They become self-respect. They become the quiet confidence to move through the world without needing to harden or withdraw.

And when children are raised with that inner steadiness, supported by *emuna*, by thoughtful guidance, and by adults who trusted the process, they carry it forward into adulthood. Not untouched by difficulty, but strengthened by it. Not rescued from life, but equipped to meet it.

Rivka Fishman grew up in Pittsburgh and holds a Psychology degree from Touro College. An award-winning educator with over 25 years in education, she coaches parents and leads workshops on bully-proofing children. She is the author of *Sara the Bucket Filler, Benny the Bucket Filler,* and *My Bucket Filling Journal.*

🌐 **thebucketfillers.com**
✉ **sarathebucketfiller@gmail.com**

Romanticizing Avodat Hashem: The Sacred Art of the Table

SHOSHANNA STEIN BENARROCH

What do romanticizing *Avodat Hashem*, tablescaping, and *Purim* have to do with one another? On the surface, they may seem unrelated, even unnecessary. We are rarely taught that beauty, atmosphere, intention, or aesthetic care are essential parts of spiritual life. We are taught how to do *mitzvot*, when to do them, and what is required, but not always how to live inside them. And yet, *Purim*, perhaps more than any other *chag*, invites us to ask a deeper question: what happens when joy, physicality, creativity, and intention are not distractions from holiness, but pathways to it? What if the way we set a table, prepare a space, and romanticize our moments is not extra, but central to how we experience our relationship with *Hashem*?

The whole point of creation, of this complex and intricate system *Hashem* created, is to have a living relationship with mankind. *Hashem* desires a deep, meaningful relationship with us, and He gave us *Torah* and *mitzvot* as a structure, a set of rules and rhythms, that allow us to connect with Him on a very deep and holy level.

But that does not mean that the relationship stops there. When we are not doing something explicitly ritualistic, we do not lose the opportunity to invite *Hashem* into our lives. *Hashem* already exists everywhere and in everything. The missing link is not *Hashem*'s presence, but our ability to open space within ourselves to invite Him in, to include Him, to ask Him to participate, and to acknowledge His divine hand in the moments and details of our lives.

The *mitzvot* are the doorway, but the relationship itself is meant to permeate every part of life. We are obligated not only to follow the structure *Hashem* gave us, but to actively invite Him into the spaces where structure is less defined, into moments that feel mundane, quiet, or purely physical.

Hashem exists everywhere, regardless of whether a space is beautiful or not. Holiness is not dependent on aesthetics. But holiness and cleanliness go together. Cleanliness and purity are not only physical concepts; they are part of the ladder that leads toward *kedushah*. A clean space is already an invitation for holiness, and a space prepared intentionally and aesthetically creates a deeper opening, allowing something inside us to soften and hold space.

This inner opening invites the feminine and the *Shekhinah*, *Hashem* as He is revealed within the world. Physicality and spirituality are deeply connected. The way we prepare the physical world directly affects the kind of spiritual presence it can receive.

This invitation to connect with *Hashem* exists at all times and is not limited to public acts of worship. Even in private moments, the invitation is waiting. We learn that a table is like a *Mizbeach*, a place where we gather, feed our families, learn *Torah*, and bless *Hashem*. The table is never neutral. It is a place where holiness can be invited, held, and revealed.

Tablescaping is not about luxury, perfection, or impressing others. It is about creating a vessel. The way a table is set, the care taken, and the intention behind it all become part of the *avodah*.

Creating a beautiful table does not require expensive items or elaborate design. It requires using whatever you have, with everything you have, infused with love, intention, and joy. When the table is prepared with the awareness that it is a *Mizbeach*, it becomes an act of consciously inviting the *Shekhinah* into the home.

This is why small choices matter. Cloth napkins instead of paper. Real glasses instead of disposable ones. Flowers from the yard. Palm leaves gathered outside. Candles placed with care. These are not decorative choices; they are relational ones. They change the energy at the table and how people arrive, speak, listen, and feel.

When a space is prepared with intention, the atmosphere shifts. The table becomes a place where people are more present, more open, and more connected.

Purim itself is defined by the *seudah*. While we put so much creativity and effort into *mishloach manot*, the *seudah* is meant to be one of the most elevated moments of the day, and the table becomes the focal point of our *avodah*. Preparing it beautifully is not extra; it is essential. A feast prepared for a king requires intention, readiness, and care, and this is how we invite the *Shekhinah* in.

Simple choices elevate the experience. Name cards create presence. Notes or personal messages create connection. Interactive elements, adjusted for age, show care and thoughtfulness. Displaying food beautifully, arranging dishes with abundance and joy, and adding whimsy through costumes, toys, or playful elements reflect the spirit of *Purim*. Using what you already have, with creativity and intention, allows joy to become a vessel for holiness rather than a distraction.

Ultimately, this is not about centerpieces or place cards. It is about presence.

Hashem created a world in order to dwell within it, and within us. The *mitzvot* give structure to that relationship, but the invitation continues in how we live and how much space we are willing to make.

Purim reminds us that *Hashem* is often found in the details, in what appears ordinary, playful, even hidden. When we elevate the *seudah*, we are not adding something external. We are revealing what is already there.

Romanticizing our *mitzvot* and our moments is a practice of awareness. It is learning to notice, to invite, and to make space, not only on *Purim*, but on *Shabbat* and throughout the *chagim* as well. When we approach these moments with love, intention, and *kavannah*, the physical world becomes more than functional. It becomes a vessel for a relationship. And in that space, something deeper is allowed to breathe.

Shoshanna Stein Benarroch is a teacher, artist, and mentor whose *chizuk* radiates from a deep awareness of *Hashem's* love. Founder of the "*Ki Tov* Project", she inspires others to seek divine goodness in every moment and see *Hashem* everywhere.

🇫 📷 **@MySoCalledJewishLife**

Real Coffee Talk

with Chaya Ben Baruch & Jodi Samuels

EXCLUSIVELY TO HER TRIBE MAGAZINE

Some women carry stories that cannot be summarized in a headline.

This Real Coffee Talk brings together Chaya Ben Baruch and Jodi Samuels, two women whose lives appear very different on the surface, yet feel deeply connected once you listen closely.

Both are mothers raising families while carrying leadership far beyond their own homes, each with her own unique perspective. Both are builders of people, initiatives, and spaces that did not exist before them. Both spent formative years in New York. Both faced loss that reshaped their prayers, refined their priorities, and redefined what strength looks like in real life. Later, each was entrusted with children whose lives called for a deeper level of presence, resilience, and responsibility.

This is not a conversation about overcoming. It is a conversation about becoming.

Chaya Ben Baruch

Chaya's life is shaped by unexpected turns. Born a twin and raised in New York in a traditional but complex Jewish home, she grew up moving between worlds of belonging and searching. At that stage of her life, she lived under a different name.

As a young woman, she left everything familiar and moved to Alaska, a place of silence and extremes that allowed her to become someone new. There, she studied biology and was drawn to sea otters, noticing how otter mothers care for their babies in the water for an entire year. During that time, she stepped

PHOTO BY DAVE BENDER

away from the Jewish world. Alaska is also where she met her husband, the man she fondly calls "Mr. Blue Eyes."

Her life includes marriage, miscarriages that reshaped her *tefillah*, loss, and a divorce she never expected. She recalls going alone into the Alaskan forest, practicing *hitbodedut*, and crying out to *Hashem* that she could not carry any more.

Her pregnancy with her son was extremely difficult, marked by constant nausea and IV infusions every few days. Throughout that pregnancy, she prayed only for a live baby. When he was born, she sensed immediately, through a mother's intuition, that he had Down syndrome. Before any diagnosis, she bonded with her child, not with a condition. She was told, "Just take him home and love him."

Later, Chaya made another unexpected decision. She adopted a baby girl with Down syndrome so her son would not grow up alone. The baby's parents

placed her in Chaya's arms and never returned. Over time, families from across Israel began reaching out to her. Parents seeking to place babies with special needs for adoption, and families hoping to adopt, found their way to Chaya. Without intending to, she became a quiet matchmaker.

Alongside raising her family, Chaya also built a bee business that grew out of kindness. What began as a simple act of care became a space that offers people with Down syndrome dignity, responsibility, and meaningful participation.

Like the story of *Queen Esther*, much of Chaya's life reveals its purpose only in hindsight. These are moments when *Hashem* seemed hidden, yet was guiding every turn.

Jodi Samuels

Originally from Johannesburg, before moving to Israel, Jodi lived in nine cities and twenty-seven apartments. A passionate traveler, she has visited 104 countries, and the number continues to grow. After making aliyah in 2014, she joked,"G-d, give me coffee for the things I can deal with, and wine for everything else."

It is a line that captures her perfectly. Grounded, humorous, and deeply realistic about life.

Jodi Samuels is not someone who waits for permission.

PHOTO: COURTESY OF JODI SAMUELS

47

PHOTO: COURTESY OF JODI SAMUELS

Long before she became an author, activist, or public speaker, she was already focused on impact. While others were partying, she was planning. She sleeps only four hours a night, and every morning she wakes up asking one question: How can I make a difference today?

That question led her into leadership roles across four cities and into the lives of tens of thousands of people searching for connection and belonging. As the founder of Jewish International Connection, Jodi created a global Jewish home away from home, helping young professionals find community, Jewish identity, and love. More than 154 marriages began through the communities and connections she built.

Her most defining transformation began in a hospital room. After experiencing miscarriages, her daughter Caila was born and diagnosed with Down syndrome. In that moment, Jodi made a decision that shaped everything that followed. She would control the narrative. Caila was not a diagnosis. She was a daughter, a human being worthy of dignity, opportunity, and expectation.

That decision came at a cost. Jodi found herself defending her daughter's right to exist, to learn, and to belong,

even within communities that spoke the language of values. She experienced rejection, exclusion, and public backlash. Once deeply shy and terrified of public speaking, she stepped forward because she understood one thing clearly. If she did not speak, nothing would change.

So she found her voice.

Today, Jodi is a disability advocate, a sought-after speaker, and the author of *Chutzpah, Wisdom and Wine: The Journey of an Unstoppable Woman*, a raw and honest memoir about playing the hand you are dealt, embracing challenge, and choosing joy without denial. She is also about to publish a new work, *Challah Wisdom and Wine: Tales from a Global Shabbat Table*.

Her mission goes far beyond her own family. Jodi challenges polite inclusion and calls for something braver. Real inclusion that opens schools, homes, communities, and hearts. The kind that demands leadership, not pity.

At the center of everything she does is one guiding belief: clarity comes from knowing your why.

Both of you experienced miscarriages that changed how you prayed. How did those losses shape what you later asked *Hashem* for?

Jodi: After having two miscarriages following the birth of my middle child, when I was pregnant with Caila, I kept praying, "Please God, give me a healthy baby." About six weeks before I gave birth, I had a mother's intuition that something was not right, even though all the doctors said everything was fine. When they took me in for the cesarean, I realized something was wrong. I prayed, "Please God, give me the strength to deal with whatever challenges are going to come."

Chaya: I have learned to see my miscarriages as a gift. Of my thirteen pregnancies, six resulted in live births. Carrying a full-term baby humbled me deeply. When my son Avichi was born, and before we knew his full condition, we were faced a week later with a baby we already loved who needed open-heart surgery. In that moment, living mattered more than Down syndrome.

Since then, I have spoken to other mothers who did not receive their child's diagnosis immediately.

Accepting our newborn was much easier that way. I felt I had a "baby who happened to have Down syndrome", not a "Down syndrome baby".

Chaya, your motherhood journey is unlike most. Can you walk us through your children, those you raised, those you welcomed through adoption and foster care, and those you carry in your heart today?

Chaya: When we made *aliyah*, I already had three children from my first marriage. They were older and chose not to come with us. Today, they live in the United States and are building their own lives.

With my husband, Yisroel, our family grew in ways I never planned. Some of our children came by birth, others through adoption and foster care, and each arrived with a story that shaped us.

Ari, our biological son, was diagnosed on the autism spectrum at twenty-five.

Dany, also our biological son, works in cyber technology for the Department of Education and volunteers with MADA.

Avichi is our biological son with Down syndrome. On his first birthday, Kirin joined our family after being given up at birth because she had Down Syndrome. She became both our daughter and Avichi's partner in life. They were married for eleven years and lived in Rechasim within the Tzohar Halev community.

Tzohar Halev, which supports people with special needs through schools, group homes, and work frameworks in Rechasim, Jerusalem, Ashkelon, and Tzfat, became central to their lives. The

PHOTO BY DAVE BENDER

From right: Chaya with her daughter Kirin and her best friend, Miri Newcome, co-founder of Neshikah Honey.

newest kindergarten in Tzfat was named Gan Avichi in his memory. Avichi passed away two and a half years ago.

Shalhevet, our first sabra, was born with Down Syndrome and left in the hospital in Tzfat shortly after birth. She lives today with a pacemaker.

Ori came to us through foster care. He was Yemenite, had Down syndrome, and serious medical challenges, including open-heart surgery. During COVID, he became critically ill, spent eleven months dependent on oxygen, and later passed away at fifteen after weeks on a respirator at Ziv Hospital in Tzfat.

Nechamie joined us at one week old, born with Down Syndrome and cystic fibrosis. She passed away at seven months from meningococcal meningitis contracted in the hospital.

Our family is built from love, loss, resilience, and faith. Some of our children are with us, some live far away, and some live on through memory and impact. Each one taught us how to hold joy and grief together and to keep choosing life.

Esther acted at the right moment, not the first moment. How have you learned when to wait and when it is time to act?

Jodi: Under stress or in difficult situations, people often get caught up in pressure or the noise around them. It's important to wait until your values and the facts align, and that is when you act.

People also need to have an honest conversation with themselves about their values. When you don't clearly know your values, decision-making breaks down. Your values can easily be influenced by your echo chamber, a parent's voice, or the expectations of society around you.

Chaya: For me, knowing when to wait and when to act comes from internal awareness. I sit with myself and wait for *Hashem*'s guidance. Over time, I have learned to recognize when it is time to move and when it is time to surrender.

Shacharit: Ori, Chaya's son, wrapped in tallit and tefillin.

PHOTO BY DAVE BENDER

Surrender was not always easy. During a very uncertain period, I was in Tzfat on *Rosh Hashanah* and heard the *Torah* reading of *Akeidat Yitzchak*. *Avraham*'s willingness to let go stayed with me, and I understood that I needed to do the same. In the end, B'H, things unfolded with clarity.

When my son Ori passed away, it took much longer. I was not angry, only deeply sad, and for some time I stopped truly communicating with *Hashem*. Then one day I experienced something very real, a literal burning bush, recorded on video. That moment reminded me that *Hashem* was asking me to speak to Him again.

Since then, I have understood that waiting and acting are part of the same relationship: listening carefully, surrendering fully, and trusting *Hashem's* timing.

I never imagined I would publicly advocate for Down syndrome, but I feel a responsibility to speak. If my voice helps a mother keep her baby long enough to bond, to let the child settle into her heart, and to choose love, then it matters.

That extra chromosome often means extra love.

What's something you've stopped doing as a mother and leader that made you more effective and more at peace?

Chaya: There is a story about a man throwing baby turtles back into the sea. Another man comes by and says, "There are thousands of these turtles washed up. You can't possibly save them all."

The first man picks up another baby turtle, gently throws it into the sea, and says, "No, but I can try to save this one."

My heart aches when I see or hear of another abandoned baby because he has Down syndrome. I try not to judge, but I do ask *Hashem* to help that baby find a forever home. In order for us to be Kirin, Shalhevet, Ori, and Nechamie's *Ima* and *Abba*, someone else had to give birth to them and give them up. We got the better end of the deal.

Jodi: The thing I stopped doing that made me a more effective leader and gave me more peace was fearing failure. You have to stop fearing failure and instead view it as a learning opportunity. Fear of failure often keeps people from moving forward at all.

You often put on your boxing gloves and feel like you have to fight all the time. Sometimes it is necessary to stop, have a glass of wine, appreciate your blessings, and adopt an attitude of gratitude. You have to step out of the role of being a mom with boxing gloves on. Sometimes you just have to scream like a good Israeli. I had never screamed before, and I had to learn how to scream.

Fear can paralyze people into inaction.

What advice would you give to families raising children with Down syndrome, and to women who want to be supportive but are unsure how to act or what to say?

Jodi: To families, I would say two things. First, your child is not the diagnosis. He or she is your child. It is important to keep that perspective and treat him or her as you would any other child in your family.

For people who do not know what to say in sensitive situations, do not say, "Your child is so cute." Nobody wants to hear that about a 15-year-old. Do not suddenly drop off gifts if you never had a relationship before. It can feel like pity. Do not avoid people, because avoidance hurts far more than you realize. Do not suddenly invite people into your life when there was no prior relationship.

Have a direct conversation. Address Down syndrome directly. Do not speak around it. The elephant in the room needs to be acknowledged.

Chaya: Give yourselves permission to feel everything. Love and fear, gratitude and grief can exist at the same time. There is no right emotional timeline. Focus on your child as a person, not a diagnosis. Build a support circle early, and remember that asking for help is wisdom.

For those who want to be supportive, you do not need the perfect words. Presence matters most. Stay. Check in. Follow the parents' lead. Support is not about saying something profound. It is about not disappearing.

Say the baby's name. Parents want to know their child will be accepted and loved.

Living in Israel brings both depth and challenge. How has life here shaped you?

Chaya: We are deeply grateful to live in Israel and to have an army that protects us so we can be with our families. I do acupuncture for soldiers in the north with Chayal's Angels and have been on the border with Lebanon and Syria weekly for almost two years.

I used to be a birth midwife. Now I am a grief midwife. Often *Hashem* sends me to a soldier or a parent of a fallen soldier, and I can look into their eyes and truly understand them.

Jodi: Living in Israel taught me *chutzpah*. "No" is the starting point of negotiation. Rules are meant to be questioned. If something does not make sense, you challenge it. Rules are the beginning, not the end.

If you were sitting across from a woman who feels behind in life, what would you want her to hear?

Jodi: For the woman who is feeling behind, I would say the following. First, behind that feeling is often a lack of clarity about what you are measuring yourself against. If you do not know what you are measuring, it is very hard to know whether you are truly behind. Without clear metrics, you cannot accurately assess where you stand.

Second, you need to know your 'why'. Knowing your why gives you focus and alignment. It takes you out of analysis paralysis and helps realign your goals, values, and expectations.

Third, each of us has the ability to impact the world in our own way. We often get caught up in thinking about being ahead or behind. When you clearly understand what matters most, you can use your abilities in a way that is meaningful to you.

Avichi z"l as a *chatan*, with Kirin—
just married.

PHOTO BY DAVE BENDER

Impact looks different for each person. This brings you back to your personal mission statement. What is your mission in life? To find it, approach it like a business. In business, you ask, "What is my reason for being?" When you define that, you have your mission statement.

When you have clarity about your mission, you know what you want to impact and why. At that point, you can ask yourself whether you are actually behind, or perhaps even ahead.

Chaya: I often quote Harav Dov Bear, also known as Winnie the Pooh. (smiles)

You are braver than you believe,
stronger than you seem,
and smarter than you think.

Chaya asks Jodi

Chaya: How do you define the shift from resilience to real growth?

Jodi: Resilience is about surviving pressure.

Real growth begins when pressure no longer defines your decisions, your identity, or your ceiling.

Resilience asks, "How do I get through this?".

Growth asks, "What am I building because of it?"

Resilience keeps you standing.

Growth moves you forward, with intention, leverage, and choice.

That is the shift.

Jodi asks Chaya

Jodi: If you had to name your true superpower, what would it be?

Chaya: When people ask how I raise five children with Down syndrome, they assume it is strength or stamina. But that is not my superpower. My superpower is simpler. I see children first. Not diagnoses. Not labels.

My heart does not divide love into biological and non-biological categories. I grew up learning to question, to think differently, and to step outside the box. That matters, because raising children with Down syndrome means rejecting narrow definitions of success.

I was the smaller, second twin and was left in the hospital while my brother went home. I do not remember it consciously, but my body remembers. I cannot separate who I am from what I lived.

I grew up surrounded by a loving, extended Jewish family, and I have learned to understand my life by connecting the dots backwards. When I do, everything makes sense.

So if I have a superpower, it is this. I give without keeping score. As a line in *Fantastic Beasts* says, "You need a giver, not a taker." I am a giver. A quiet doer. Love does not need applause. Love keeps showing up.

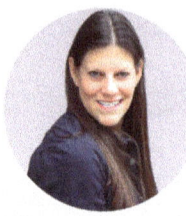

Jodi Samuels is a connector and community builder, social entrepreneur, disability advocate, keynote speaker, and author. Author of *Chutzpah, Wisdom and Wine: The Journey of an Unstoppable Woman. Challah Wisdom and Wine: Tales from a Global Shabbat Table* (coming soon).

jodisvoice.com

jodi@jicny.com

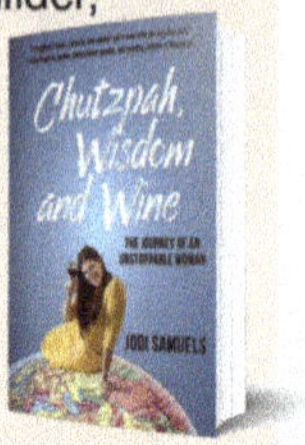
Chutzpah, Wisdom and Wine
THE JOURNEY OF AN UNSTOPPABLE WOMAN
JODI SAMUELS

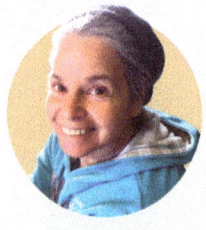

Chaya Ben Baruch is a lecturer on Down syndrome and kidney donation, an acupuncturist since 2005, a birth and grief midwife, and a self-described 'momologist'. She holds degrees in Biological Sciences and a Master's in Teaching from UAF, is a certified *Montessori* educator, fluent in English and Hebrew, and co-founder of *Neshikha*.

neshikha.com

chaya2426@gmail.com

SPONSORED

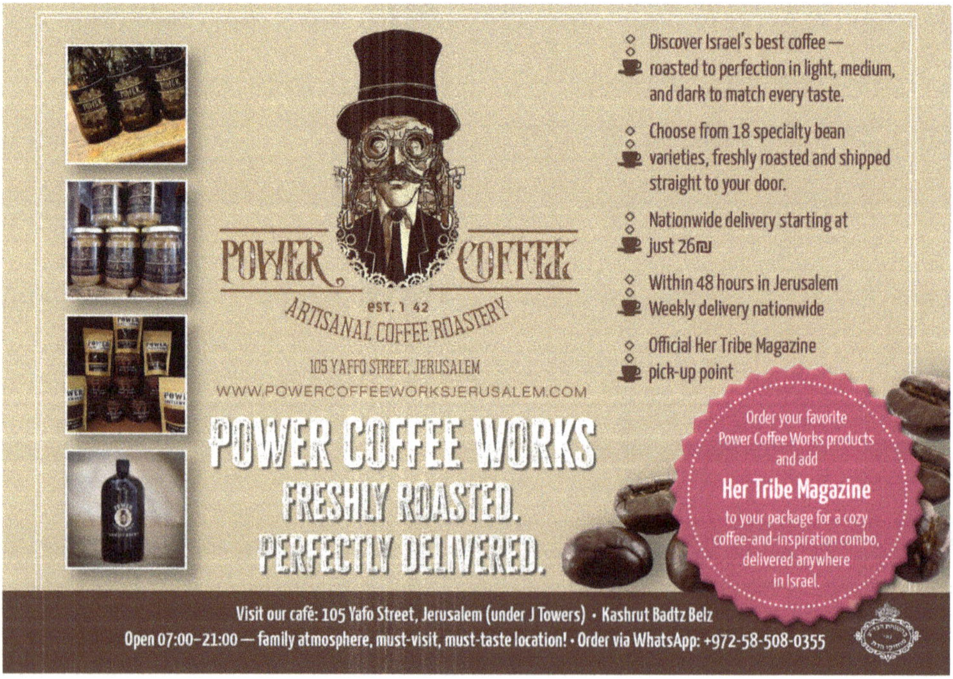
POWER COFFEE
EST. 1 42
ARTISANAL COFFEE ROASTERY
105 YAFFO STREET, JERUSALEM
WWW.POWERCOFFEEWORKSJERUSALEM.COM
POWER COFFEE WORKS
FRESHLY ROASTED.
PERFECTLY DELIVERED.
Discover Israel's best coffee — roasted to perfection in light, medium, and dark to match every taste.
Choose from 18 specialty bean varieties, freshly roasted and shipped straight to your door.
Nationwide delivery starting at just 26₪
Within 48 hours in Jerusalem
Weekly delivery nationwide
Official Her Tribe Magazine pick-up point
Order your favorite Power Coffee Works products and add
Her Tribe Magazine
to your package for a cozy coffee-and-inspiration combo, delivered anywhere in Israel.
Visit our café: 105 Yafo Street, Jerusalem (under J Towers) • Kashrut Badtz Belz
Open 07:00–21:00 — family atmosphere, must-visit, must-taste location! • Order via WhatsApp: +972-58-508-0355

A Gun, a Tzedakah Call, and the Hand of Hashem

BY SIGALIT LAREDO

It happened on an ordinary winter night—the kind of evening that should have passed quietly. Snow was falling steadily, thick enough to soften the streets and slow the world down. I had just finished work and stopped at the shopping center near my home to take care of a few simple errands: something from the pharmacy, a book for an upcoming trip. Nothing felt unusual. I didn't sense danger. I didn't know I was being followed.

I drove home, opened the garage door, and prepared to pull in. When I looked inside, I saw that the stroller had been left in my parking spot. I put the car in park, left the engine running, and opened my door to move it.

That was the moment everything changed.

From the corner of my eye, I noticed a young man in a hooded jacket approaching. He wasn't too close, and for a brief second I wondered if he might be one of my older children's friends. There was no instinctive alarm, no warning that something was wrong.

Then, without hesitation, he reached into his coat and pulled out a gun.

"Lady, get out of the car! Leave the keys in the car! Get out now!"

Shock does not arrive loudly. It freezes time. My thoughts raced through everything inside the car—my laptop from work, my purse, the suits I had just picked up from the cleaners, the cash from the bank. A practical thought flashed through my mind: *How can I just leave everything?*

As a Black Belt martial artist, a trained instinct surfaced for a split second. Could I disarm him when he got closer? But it was immediately clear that this moment was not about my skills or control.

This was a *cheshbon* far beyond anything I could understand. Only *Hashem* knew what was being weighed and what was being spared. Who knows what kind of kapara was taking place, perhaps correcting something from this life or even another.

Kapara is not a punishment.
It is mercy, sometimes
negotiating something far worse.

He moved fast, stepped closer, grabbed the shoulder of my jacket, pulled me out of the car, and shoved me toward the snowbank without hurting me. Seconds later, he was already sliding into the driver's seat. The engine roared as he disappeared into the snowy night.

They took possessions and nothing more, and I knew that was not by chance. That was Hashem in full control.

For a moment, I couldn't move. Then I thought maybe we could catch him. I ran into the house, calling my husband's name.

Upstairs, my husband had been watching our five-year-old son and his rabbi, practicing *Alef-Beit* and learning the *parsha*. When he heard the panic in my voice, he rushed downstairs.

"What happened? What's wrong?"

"He stole my car. Everything is inside— go after him!"

My husband ran outside, but it was already too late. The car was gone. We called the police, who arrived quickly. They explained that there had been a ring stealing SUVs in our area for several days. My car was exactly the model they were targeting.

Before leaving, the officers spoke to me gently. They explained that what I had experienced was traumatic and that fear, nightmares, or anxiety might surface later. They gave me the number of a psychologist and encouraged me to call if needed.

That night, when the house finally grew quiet, I said *Shema al ha-mitta* slowly, with all the words of protection. And then I slept—deeply and peacefully. No nightmares. No panic. No fear. Only a strong, steady awareness that I had been protected.

I knew without question that I had been in *Hashem's* hands the entire time.

THE HIDDEN LAYER I LEARNED LATER

There was a detail that only became clear afterward—one that reframed the entire experience.

At the exact moment the robber pointed the gun at me outside, my husband was upstairs on the phone with Rabbi Raskin, the father of the rabbi who had come to teach our son. He had called to express *hakarat hatov* and to make a *tzedakah* donation, thanking him for the care and dedication his son showed in teaching ours.

The phone call happened at the very same moment the danger unfolded.

A *mitzvah* in one place.
Protection in another.

When my husband spoke at the *Shabbat kiddush* that week, he shared what had happened and said:

"I believe with all my heart that it was the merit of *tzedakah* that protected my wife. She was not harmed, not abducted, not injured. *Hashem* watched over her."

What had felt chaotic now appeared precisely timed. What had been terrifying was, in truth, surrounded by care we could only recognize afterward.

That *Shabbat*, we sponsored a *Seudat Hoda'ah*—a public expression of gratitude for a miracle that was deeply personal.

STRENGTH THAT FOLLOWED

In the days that followed, I noticed something unexpected. Instead of feeling shaken, I felt strengthened. The fear the police had warned me about never arrived. I didn't relive the moment. I didn't feel panic taking over.

I also received calls and messages from people I would never have expected to reach out. Their warmth and genuine concern touched me deeply and strengthened my sense of *Ahavat Yisrael*. It reminded me how much quiet goodness exists between us, even when we don't always see it.

The experience deepened my awareness of *hashgacha pratit*—of how *Hashem* is present even when we do not immediately see Him. It reminded me that *mitzvot* are not abstract ideas, but living acts with real impact.

A PURIM WAY OF SEEING

Purim is the story of what is hidden. *Hashem's* name never appears in the *Megillah*, yet His presence is unmistakable.

A stroller left in the garage delayed me by seconds.
A *tzedakah* call happened at the exact moment danger appeared.
A frightening moment ended not in tragedy, but in gratitude.

That night reminded me that even in fear, *Hashem* is near. Even in chaos, He is orchestrating care. I was protected—and reminded that the hand of *Hashem* is always closer than we think.

Sigalit Laredo was born in Haifa, Israel, and raised in Montreal, Canada. She is the founder and director of JEMS, Jewish Experience Mothers & Sisters, an educator and motivational speaker in four languages, and a community leader for 30 years. She is a Black Belt Kung Fu instructor, a mother of five, and a grandmother of ten, *Baruch* Hashem.

📱 WhatsApp group: Private message to join
✉ sigylaredo@me.com
📷 @sigy_laredo
▶ @jemswithsigalitlaredo7539

SHE CHOSE LIFE

A Purim Story of Emuna, Quiet Courage, and Generations Rebuilt

Hetty Esther Lissauer-Abrahamson z"l with her daughter, Gilah Evers-Lissauer, on her wedding day.

BY GILAH EVERS-LISSAUER

When I think of my mother, the first image that comes to mind is not fear, hunger, or loss.

It is steadiness.

A woman rooted in life. A woman who built.

My mother was born in Amsterdam in 1934 into a solid Jewish family. Her parents had waited a long time for a child, and when she was born, she was deeply cherished. Four years later, her younger sister Rifka was born. Rifka did not survive the war. This was not a story my mother told. It was an absence that shaped everything that followed.

Both of her grandfathers were respected men. One was described to me by someone who had known him as a true *Talmid Chacham*. Jewish life surrounded her early childhood. Big families, warmth, community, shared purpose. Family members were active in publishing a Dutch Jewish journal for children.

My mother kept a few copies at home and loved showing them to us. It was one of the only pieces of "before" she ever allowed into our lives.

She was six years old when the war began.

She did not describe the *Shoah*. She did not recount scenes or emotions. A close friend later explained that survivors did not speak about feelings or memories. It was simply too excruciating. Over time, I understood something deeper. My mother knew when to speak, and when silence was strength. She understood that constantly returning to the terrible past would give it power.

Like *Queen Esther*, she carried what needed to remain hidden and revealed herself through action.

As a child during the war, she remembered playing outside with other children, watching ants and small insects. These were fragile memories of life continuing. The impression I carry

is that the children lived day by day, alive because someone made sure they stayed alive. Often, it was women who took care of them, watched over them, fed them, and kept them moving forward.

My mother went through the war with her own mother by her side. By the end of the war, that presence was gone.

One object my mother carried with her through everything was her own mother's small suitcase, the one used for the *mikveh*. I don't know how it survived the war, but it did. She held onto it all her life as a symbol of *taharat hamishpacha*, of life continuing, of family being rebuilt, and of new generations coming into the world despite everything.

After the war, my mother was brought to Odessa and faced an impossible decision at just ten years old. Return to Holland or go to *Eretz Yisrael*. Her heart longed for Israel. She spoke about that longing more than once. But she did not know if her father was still alive. And so

A chatuna in Crown Heights — Son Osher Levy, kallah Chaya, and family, B"H.

1942: Hetty Esther with her sister Beppy (Rivka), z"l.

She often spoke about the births she had helped with, every Jewish baby a quiet victory.

Family was everything to her. "When you are with family, you are safe," she used to say. She built her home around that belief. We were three daughters. She wanted a larger family, but accepted what Hashem gave her with gratitude.

Her *chesed* extended far beyond our home. When I was eleven, a close friend lost her mother. My mother gathered that girl into our family, bringing her along on vacations, including her in daily life. Years later, that girl's brother became my husband. One act of kindness shaped an entire future.

she chose to wait, believing that if he was alive, she would find him in Holland, not in Israel.

That choice was an act of *emuna*.

She waited. And she was right.

She found her father. Looking back, this was one of the clearest moments of *hashgacha pratit* in her life, a quiet decision that shaped everything that came after.

Life after the war was not simple. Her father remarried, and the home was not a kind one. Still, she moved forward. She finished school, worked in a Jewish office, and later became a nurse. Learning mattered deeply to her. When my youngest sister was five, my mother went back to study and became a teacher for nurses, later working in administration for nursing schools connected to hospitals. She loved her work, and people loved her.

My mother celebrated life every single day. That was her *Purim*. She loved hosting guests, baking, and giving. Every year she made a large apple cake for a Jewish market in Amsterdam, not for recognition, but because it brought people together.

Purim was never just another Jewish holiday in our home. My mother passed away on *Purim*, 1984, at the age of 49. Since then, besides observing *Purim*, our family has an additional custom. A *yahrzeit seudah*. Not a meal of sadness, but one of gratitude. A declaration that we are here.

Haman fell.

Hitler, *yemach shemo*, fell.

And her life is the proof.

I realized that to its full extent at the *chupa* of one of our younger children.

Baruch Hashem, I am sure my mother was looking down on us with much *nachas.*

My mother's name was Hetty (Esther) Lissauer-*Abraham*son.

Another moment stayed with her deeply: our oldest child was born on the *yahrzeit* of her father—one generation closing, another opening on the same day. To her, this was *Hashem* quietly showing that life continues.

My mother had an illness, as a nurse she knew what that meant. Months before her *petira*, she spoke to my husband, Shimon, she told him which *pasuk* she wanted on her *Matseva.*

As a rabbi and son-in-law, he did that for her. "*Tsadik Hashem Bechol Derachav*". (*Hashem* is righteous in all His ways.)
—(Psalms 145:17)

She lived with deep belief in the *Geulah.* Not as an idea, but as a way of standing in the world. Her faith was not loud. It was steady. She showed it by choosing life again and again.

In her final days, that choice never left her.

On the way to the hospital, in the ambulance, she could barely speak. Her strength was almost gone. She touched my sister's hand and pointed outside. Narcissus flowers were in bloom. Even then, she noticed *Hashem's* creation.

Even then, she chose life.

She was thankful for the miracle of being alive, "*Bayamim Hahem Bazman Hazeh*". ("In those days, at this very time.")

She expressed it by building a family, opening her home, and keeping her heart open.

She chose my name, Gilah, joy. Not as a reaction to the past, but as a declaration for the future. Joy as resistance. Joy as faith.

She chose life. And because of that, so did we.

Gilah Evers-Lissauer

Besides being a devoted mother to a large family, Gilah, as a Chabad *Shlucha* in Amsterdam, enjoys connecting with women around her *Shabbos* table. Be it over a meal or a cup of tea. She feels living close to her children and grandchildren is a gift from *Hashem*. She views working on personal *Geulah* as a meaningful and ongoing *Avodah.*

✉ **judasmam@gmail.com**

WHEN THE STORY TURNS INSIDE OUT:
Emotional Healing

ART "BERESHEET" BY EVA BIBAS

BY YEHUDIT SARAH WALLER

Purim teaches us that the world is not what it appears to be. What looks blocked may be unfolding. What feels painful may be part of a deeper healing. What seems hidden may be where *Hashem* is most present.

I was reminded of this recently during a quiet morning conversation in my *Lev Emuna* women's group on Zoom. A woman shared that she was struggling at work with a colleague who, in her eyes, seemed determined to undermine her. She spoke with anger and exhaustion. She felt unseen, threatened, and afraid that her efforts would never be acknowledged.

We listened. No one rushed to offer advice. No one analyzed the other person. We stayed with what was alive inside her.

There was a time when I did not know how to do that. I once believed that the answers to life's challenges lived outside of me. I was a devoted consumer of self help books, turning their pages for guidance on relationships, parenting, spiritual growth, and professional struggles. Those books didn't remain neatly arranged on shelves. They followed me into the messiness of life.

There was the humiliation of discovering that one child's friends had egged our house. There was the discomfort of explaining to family that my husband and I could no longer eat non kosher food. There was the ache of my oldest child leaving home, stepping into independence while I stood quietly on the threshold.

With time, I learned that wisdom and the path to healing does not only come from reading. It comes from presence. From allowing emotions to be felt rather than managed. From being heard without judgment.

In one group conversation, a woman shared the pain of wanting to be married and watching the years pass. The longing sat heavily in the room. No one tried to make it smaller. Instead, we asked gentle questions. What story are you telling yourself about this waiting? Are you judging yourself? Is it possible to experience moments of joy even while this desire remains unmet?

There is a Baal Shem Tov teaching that we are where our thoughts are. That idea alone can turn everything upside down. Like *Purim*, it reveals that the real drama does not unfold on the surface. It unfolds within. As she spoke, her face softened. Nothing external changed, yet something inside her shifted.

Then it was my turn.

I spoke about a friendship that had been weighing on me. I love this friend deeply, yet I often feel silenced around her. She speaks with certainty, dismisses my ideas, and fills the space so completely that I disappear inside myself. A simple shared project had stirred something old and familiar: frustration, hurt, the ache of not being heard.

In the past, I would have spiraled. I would have dissected her behavior, questioned my own personality, replayed the same inner refrain: Why can't I speak up? Why do I disappear?

This time, I didn't want advice. I didn't want reassurance. I wanted to meet my emotions honestly.

I closed my eyes and breathed. I allowed the feelings to surface without pushing them away. I noticed where they lived in my body. I imagined holding them with the same compassion a mother offers a child who has come home wounded.

And then something loosened.

The circumstances did not change. My friend did not suddenly become different. But the story I carried about myself softened its grip.

That is *Purim* healing.

The decree still exists, but its meaning reverses. The external no longer dictates the internal. What once felt threatening loses its power. Hidden kindness emerges. A quiet sense of alignment returns.

Later that day, I went for a long walk to my favorite pond. I noticed a lightness in my step. I felt open rather than braced. I could see my friend more clearly, without needing her to meet every emotional need. I remembered what I genuinely appreciated about her: her energy, her humor, her generosity, the laughter we share.

When we met later for dinner, the interaction unfolded with surprising ease. When she dismissed one of my ideas, I responded simply and clearly, without tension or collapse. She laughed, and the moment passed. What once felt charged now felt ordinary.

Purim reminds us that transformation does not always arrive with drama. Sometimes it comes quietly, through a shift in perception. Sometimes the miracle is internal.

There are moments when the pain we hold is not personal, but collective. On days when the news feels unbearable, when suffering feels too large to carry, I return to prayer. Not as performance, but as a relationship. I speak honestly. I allow grief to be present. I send love where I cannot send answers.

Redemption, like the *Purim* story itself, often unfolds without fanfare. *Hashem's* name may be hidden, but His presence is unmistakable to those who learn to listen.

Lately, I have been reflecting on beginnings. On mornings. On that quiet time when the sky is still dim and the birds begin to stir. There is something tender about those moments, something full of possibility. A chance to set intention. To speak softly to *Hashem*. To begin again.

Purim teaches us that masks will fall. That what appears chaotic may be Divinely ordered. That healing often comes not from changing the world, but from allowing the heart to soften and see differently.

We are not promised a life without struggle. But we are promised that we are never alone within it.

And sometimes, that is miracle enough.

Yehudit Sarah Waller is a *baalas teshuva*, proud mother and devoted grandmother. She is a retired educator, writer, *Lev Emuna Therapy* Facilitator and *Nurtured Heart Approach®* Advanced Trainer and Coach. She is passionate about providing guidance to help people grow to their greatest potential.

✉ janet.waller@gmail.com

ART "ESA AINAI" BY SHEVA CHAYA   SHEVACHAYA.COM

When Emuna Is Quiet and Everything Changes

BY SUZANNE SACKSTEIN

There are moments in life when you think you understand how things are supposed to unfold. You make plans. You imagine timelines. You assume that if you do everything "right," life will follow the order you expect.

When we got married, we had a plan. We assumed we would build our life step by step, first marriage, then children, all within the timeframe we had imagined. Like many couples, we believed that starting a family would simply happen.

After six months of trying without success, we went to see a doctor. We were told that everything looked fine and that we shouldn't worry. We were advised to relax, to go away, and to trust that it would all happen naturally, in the right time.

But time passed. And then more time passed.

It took us four years to have our first children. Four years of waiting, hoping, and living with a quiet fear that maybe this would never happen for us. During that time, many of our friends were already on their second pregnancies. Life moved forward for everyone else, while we continued to wait to start our family.

Infertility is a deeply lonely experience. Even when you are surrounded by people, it can feel isolating. There is a pain that is difficult to explain unless you have lived it, the constant awareness of what you don't yet have, and the uncertainty of whether you ever will.

At one point during our journey, we spoke to a rabbi who gave us advice that stayed with me and shaped the way I understood *emuna* during this time. He told us not to take on anything extra. Not to bargain with *Hashem*. Not to think in terms of, "If I do this, then *Hashem* will give me children."

Hashem does not need us to negotiate with Him.

He explained that attaching conditions, more *Tehillim*, more promises, more pressure, can actually make the experience harder. What we were asked to do was much simpler, and much deeper, to continue doing what we were already doing properly, and to trust that nothing is random. This journey belonged to us as a couple, regardless of where the medical issue lay.

That idea brought a quiet kind of *emuna*. Not loud. Not dramatic. Just steady.

Then, after four years, everything changed.

When I found out that I was pregnant, my first feeling was disbelief. It didn't feel real. After that came overwhelming gratitude, to *Hashem*, to the people who supported us, and to my husband, who carried so much of my sadness and did everything he could to keep me positive through the hardest moments.

And then we found out it was triplets.

There are no words that truly capture that moment. It was beyond overwhelming, and at the same time, filled with gratitude. What we had waited for so long for came suddenly, multiplied beyond anything we had imagined. Quiet *emuna*, and then a life completely transformed.

Not long after the triplet sons were born, we were blessed again. Just one year and ten days later, we had another precious son and then eighteen months later we had our last child and only daughter. At one point, we had five children under the age of three. It was a blur, exhausting, intense, and filled with constant reminders of *Hashem's brachot*.

Looking back, I see how much this journey reshaped me. Before everything we went through, I always imagined having a career first and then a family. After our struggle, I gained a profound appreciation for family. My children never detracted from my individual aspirations. They clarified them. They taught me what truly mattered.

Through every step, I see *hashgacha pratit*. Even during the lows, when it didn't feel that way at all. And especially afterward, when I could finally look back and see how *Hashem* was guiding us, even when we couldn't understand the path.

Our experience also changed the way we wanted to live beyond our own family. After going through infertility, which was emotionally isolating and financially stressful, we kept asking ourselves how we could play it forward.

A few years after our children were born, someone in our community approached us about helping another couple struggling to pay for their infertility treatment. After a few phone calls, we managed to raise the money they needed. That moment answered the question we had been carrying with us, and that is how the Malka Ella Fertility Fund was born.

Today, the Malka Ella Fertility Fund, based in South Africa, supports Jewish couples through the emotional, financial, and physical challenges of infertility. Since inception the fund has assisted over 400 couples fulfill their dreams of having a family. While not always in their desired timeframe, or in the way they imagined, almost all of these couples have been blessed with children in *Hashem's* time.

If I were speaking to another woman going through infertility, sister to sister, I would say this. It is an extremely difficult journey. It can feel painfully lonely. Please try to find support wherever you can, people you feel safe with, people who truly care about you, and people you trust.

At the same time, focus on your marriage. Focus on yourself. Focus on your overall well-being. These things matter, even when everything feels overshadowed by longing.

And please G-d, in the right time, *Hashem* will give you the child you are so desperately hoping and praying for.

Emuna is often lived without knowing where it is leading, and then, like Purim itself, the story quietly turns over, years of no children followed by three at once, and then more.

Suzanne Sackstein, PhD is the founding director of the Malka Ella Fertility Fund (South Africa). Drawing from her own fertility journey, she is dedicated to helping Jewish couples living in South Africa navigate infertility through financial assistance, emotional support, halachic guidance, and genetic testing. Suzanne, runs the Fund together with her husband and lives in Johannesburg, SA.

🌐 **malkaella.co.za**
✉ **info@malkaella.co.za**

Trusting the Unknown: Bitachon, Leadership, and Becoming

BY MALKIE KOZLOVA

My story is the story of a rebellious daughter, the kind of story that, when people hear it, makes them exhale and think, "Thank G-d, that wasn't me." I'm not saying this from a place of victimhood, and I'm not saying it to judge myself. I'm saying it because almost everyone has stood at a moment in life where the path disappeared, where direction felt impossible, and answers simply didn't exist. My Jewish journey grew out of those moments. It is a refusal to believe that there are no answers, and an acceptance that sometimes the deepest truth lives inside uncertainty itself. It is a story about learning to trust the unknown. Let's begin.

For as long as I can remember, I carried a quiet, aching feeling that I didn't belong anywhere.

I grew up moving between places and countries. Moscow never felt like home. Neither did London, where I went to high school, or Rome, where I went to university, or my family, my schools, or the communities I passed through. I didn't have words for it then, but something inside me was always searching. I thought I was looking for justice, for meaning, for answers about what was wrong with the world. Only much later did I understand that my soul had been searching for *Hashem* the entire time.

As a teenager, my response to pain was action. I volunteered, protested, read endlessly, and argued with everyone. I believed that if enough people cared enough, the world would change. My radical passion for justice became my identity. It gave me direction, but not peace. No matter how much I did, something still felt hollow.

The turning point came quietly, something almost accidental, which was a photograph. My great-great-grandfather is sitting *shiva* for my great-grandmother, the woman I am named after. I didn't even know what *shiva* was. I didn't know I had a Jewish story. And yet, the moment I began asking questions, everything shifted. My radical passion didn't disappear, it transformed. My hunger for justice became a hunger for truth. And that truth led me straight into Judaism.

I went from zero to one hundred, not because someone convinced me, but because my *neshama* woke up. And once it woke up, there was no way to silence it. I learned. I walked long distances to *Beit Chabad* in Rome. I showed up when no one expected me, often alone. It was hard. There were moments of rejection, moments of quiet humiliation, moments when I felt painfully unseen. But every one of them softened me. Every one of them stripped away ego and taught me balance.

Eventually, a rabbi looked at me and said something simple that changed everything: You should go to Israel. And so I went, with nothing. No plan, no safety net, no guarantees. It wasn't a sacrifice. It was the first time in my life I felt I was walking toward my purpose. I trusted *Hashem* in confusion, one step at a time. I learned that *bitachon* isn't feeling calm, it's trusting that the hardest moments of your life are shaping your mission, even when you don't understand how.

This journey wasn't linear. There were intense phases, broken expectations, a broken engagement, a marriage that didn't last, and an abusive relationship after the divorce. I don't call these mistakes. I don't believe in that language anymore. My story isn't about failure. It's about *Hashem* arranging everything precisely so I could become the woman I am today.

The breaking point became the beginning of clarity. For the first time, I stopped and asked myself real questions: Who am I? What does

PHOTO BY @OH.SHOSHI.AVI

somewhere, and the way to make that beginning "kosher" is to support each other through it. The platform is a startup that helps and supports Russian-speaking Jews on these journeys.

If you've ever felt rejected, unloved, or out of place, I see you. I was you.

My life didn't begin when I fit into someone else's expectations. It began when I stopped resisting the uncertainty and trusted that *Hashem* was guiding me, even when I couldn't see where.

That trust changed everything.

Hashem want from me right now? Those questions changed how I make decisions. Instead of rushing forward, I learned to pause. To breathe. To listen. To ask smaller, gentler questions. Does this bring me closer to the truth? Does this align with who I am becoming? Is this coming from fear or from trust?

Slowly, something settled inside me.

Today, my mission is rooted in that clarity. I work, I build, I lead, but I do it differently now: with dignity, with awareness, and with compassion for women who are searching the way I once was. I help create spaces where Judaism feels accessible, honest, and human. No humiliation. No unanswered questions. Just real connection.

The project I lead, called *Am Olam*, responds to the pain many people feel around Judaism's "burden." *Yiddishkeit* is not supposed to be a popularity contest or a test. We are all beginning

Malkie Kozlova lives in Jerusalem, Israel. She holds a Bachelor's degree in Political Science and a Master's degree in Business. She is the CEO and co-founder of *Am Olam*, a digital platform creating accessible, dignified pathways to Jewish life for Russian-speaking Jews worldwide.

- @malkie.kozlova
- malka-kozlova-9a67a9378
- olam.am
  (in Russian—*use an AI translator*)

THE BRIDGE BETWEEN SHABBOS AND THE WEEK AHEAD:

MELAVA *Malka*

BY SARA GOCHBERG

The moment everything shifted wasn't dramatic.

I was standing in my kitchen on *Motzaei Shabbos* in November 2018. The *chagim* were behind us, winter was approaching, and I was thinking about the week ahead.

After an entire *Shabbos* of challah, the last thing I wanted was to wash again. For me, *Motzaei Shabbos* meant a quick cleanup and moving on, not another meal.

I'll be honest: I had never been a *Melava Malka* person. Growing up, it wasn't part of our *Motzei Shabbos* routine.

Motzaei Shabbos often meant a snack, something light. There wasn't this concept of washing for a fourth meal to honor the departing *Shabbos* Queen.

And I was carb-phobic, wash-phobic, and *bentch*-phobic—a trifecta many women will recognize.

But that night, something whispered: *What if this mitzvah could bring more bracha into our lives?*

THE MOMENTUM THAT MADE IT POSSIBLE

Years earlier, during a conversation about Shabbos, my aunt once told me, "If you're only washing for two meals and not the third, you're missing something." Her words stayed with me. I took them to heart and committed to being careful about all three meals, even on short winter afternoons, when it would have been easy to let it slide.

So I thought: if I can do that, I can try *Melava Malka.*

That *Motzaei Shabbos* felt like the

perfect trial run. I wasn't committing for life. Just starting.

THAT FIRST WEEK

I kept it simple. Grilled cheese—a family favorite with mustard, tomatoes, cheese, and oregano. I posted a photo with a simple caption: "What Are You Washing On?"

By morning, my phone was buzzing. "I want to join." "What are you washing on next week?"

I didn't realize I was starting anything. I thought my recipe was going viral.

That one grilled cheese became the spark for what grew into the *Melava Malka Challenge.* A community-driven initiative encouraging people to try washing for *Melava Malka,* whether weekly or even just once.

A GRADUAL, REAL TRANSFORMATION

The first couple of years felt personal. I shared quietly, mostly on my own page. Some weeks I stopped and started again. Most of my family wasn't washing with me, and that was okay.

Then something shifted.

We created a WhatsApp group and an email list. People began sharing stories, encouraging one another, and making the mitzvah feel warm, doable, and real. I discovered how many people were already washing—quietly and faithfully—with beautiful family traditions of their own.

Later, we held a *Melava Malka* learning series with Rabbi Reichman, who said something that shifted how I saw this: "Sometimes a *mitzvah* becomes *your*

mitzvah." When I shared that with my husband, he laughed and said, "Of course mine had to be about food!"

I realized this *mitzvah* was far deeper than I had known.

As I learned more, I began adding intention: a hot drink, leaving the tablecloth on, not rushing to "put *Shabbos* away." These small acts became reminders that *Shabbos* doesn't disappear the moment the stars come out.

After October 7, we began dedicating our *Melava Malka* efforts as a *zechus* for our hostages, *IDF* soldiers, and all those impacted by the war. Doing the *mitzvah* with that intention gave it even deeper meaning.

Today, in its eighth year, the focus is *achdus*, sharing *Melava Malka* in homes and communities. The *mitzvah* is elevated when it's experienced together.

That sense of togetherness is what makes this initiative so special. The friendships that form, and the way women from different countries, backgrounds, and walks of life come together around one *mitzvah*—that's where the real magic happens. I'm a people person at heart, and I love creating spaces where connections can grow naturally. Our supporters, the Ambassadors, have played a central role in this. By carrying the message into their own communities, they're what truly allowed the initiative to grow.

WHAT CHANGED

My work life is busy, and the temptation is always there: *Shabbos* ends, check my phone, jump back in.

But *Melava Malka* forces a pause.

HOW TO BE PART OF IT

The *Melava Malka* Challenge is simply an invitation to try washing for *Melava Malka*, weekly, occasionally, or even just once.

Those who wish to connect can find inspiration and practical guidance through the *Melava Malka* Challenge community.

Resources and updates are shared via:

🔲 **@melavamalkachallenge**

✉ **melavamalkachallenge@gmail.com**

🔲 **WhatsApp groups and status**

A short resource guide, *Melava Malka* Done Right, created in partnership with *Halacha for Today*, is available upon request.

Washing, keeping the tablecloth on, holding a warm cup of tea—all of it reminds me: I don't have to rush yet. Sunday will come soon enough. For now, I'm choosing to carry *Shabbos* forward.

WHAT IS MELAVA MALKA?

Melava Malka means escorting the Queen, the meal eaten after *Shabbos* to honor the departing *Shabbos* Queen. It is the bridge between the holiness we've just experienced and the week ahead.

Chazal teach that *Melava Malka* nourishes the *luz* bone, a spiritual bone from which resurrection will take place. Because it is spiritual in nature, it is nourished only through this *mitzvah*.

Melava Malka is also known as a powerful *segulah* for *refuah, parnassah,*

arichas yamim, children, easier labor, protection, and *yeshuos*.

MAKING IT REAL

Start small. Try it once.

Plan ahead during *Shabbos* prep and keep it simple. Having something ready makes all the difference.

Many have customs such as leaving the tablecloth on, singing *zemiros*, or sharing *divrei Torah*. Hot food or a hot drink is especially meaningful for a *refuah* for the body and the *neshamah*.

Try it one week, and your *Motzaei Shabbos* may never feel the same. It becomes less about the end of *Shabbos* and more about the bridge into the week.

Do it with your family. Invite friends. Bring it into your community. Once you experience *Motzaei Shabbos* through *Melava Malka*, it's hard to go back.

When we escort the *Shabbos* Queen with intention, we're saying the holiness doesn't end when the stars come out. We're carrying it forward, and inviting the *brachos* to pull up a chair at our table.

Sara Gochberg is a business advisor, AI architect and the accidental founder of the *Melava Malka* Challenge. Drawing on her business background, she raises awareness of this *mitzvah* and inspires meaningful participation.

ART "MIRIAM'S DRUM ON KLAF" / BY SHEVA CHAYA / SHEVACHAYA.COM

Az Yashir: The Women Who Sang First

Miriam, *Shabbos Shirah*, and the Faith That Flowers

BY KEREN MILLER

Kriat Yam Suf is one of the most dramatic and awe-inspiring moments in Jewish history. The sea split, the impossible became reality, and an enslaved nation walked to freedom on dry land. Yet beyond the miracle itself lies a deeper message, one that speaks directly to the heart of every Jewish woman.

The *Shabbos* on which *Parashat Beshalach* is read is known as *Shabbos Shirah*, the Sabbath of Song. It is the moment when *Moshe Rabbeinu* led *Bnei Yisrael* in singing the Song of Praise and Exultation to G-d following the crossing of the *Yam Suf*.

The special song *Moshe* composed is "*Az Yashir*", and his sister, *Miriam HaNeviah*, also led the women in song and praise after the crossing of the sea.

Significantly, *Az Yashir* is written in the future tense, teaching that *Moshe* not only sang then, but will lead us again at the final redemption. Until that day, we recite this song daily, expressing gratitude even while redemption is still unfolding.

Shirah is more than music; it is an outpouring of jubilation that rises from the deepest recesses of the soul. At the Sea of Reeds, the Jewish people witnessed revelations so great that even the prophets did not behold them. The heavens opened, angels were seen, and even the simplest handmaiden could point and declare with certainty, "*Ze Keili*" (This is my G-d). Faith was no longer abstract; it was visible and undeniable.

Yet *Moshe* begins the song with humility. Aware of the limits of human understanding, the *Torah* leaves deliberate "blank spaces" within the Song, teaching us that the Infinite cannot be fully grasped. There are moments when faith means leaving space, remaining silent and anchored to trust, even when answers elude us.

THE WORD "AZ" ITSELF CARRIES A POWERFUL TRANSFORMATION.

Moshe once cried out in pain, "*Mei'az*. From the time I came to *Pharaoh*, things became worse." Now, with that same word, *Az*, he sings praise. This teaches us that faith reaches its highest level not only when we thank *Hashem* for salvation, but when we recognize that even the suffering itself was purposeful, refining us and leading us toward our destiny as a nation worthy of covenant, responsibility, and light.

The sea did not split immediately. The people stood trapped between terror and uncertainty until one act of courage, stepping forward, brought redemption. Faith preceded the miracle.

And standing there was *Miriam*.

MIRIAM: TURNING BITTERNESS INTO HOPE

The name *Miriam* is rooted in *maror*, bitterness. Yet through her unwavering faith, *Miriam* transformed bitterness into renewal and life.

From where did *Miriam* obtain these tambourines? Even while still enslaved, she prepared them, certain that redemption would come. She refused despair and chose hope and trust.

When salvation arrived, *Miriam* led the women not only in song, but in movement and joy. She teaches us that faith is not passive. *Miriam* danced and the women joined her. She prepared instruments while still in exile. It was *Miriam's* trust in *Hashem* that brought about salvation even when the future was unclear.

MIRACLES THEN, AND NOW

We may not see seas split before us, but each woman faces her own crossing:

A child she worries about.
A challenge with no visible solution.
A prayer still waiting for an answer.

Sometimes the miracle is not the removal of hardship, but the realization that through it we grew, revealed strength, and discovered our purpose.

ART "MAKAMAT WOMEN'S ENSEMBLE" BY SHEVA CHAYA | SHEVACHAYA.COM

THE FEMININE STRENGTH OF *EMUNA*

Our bondage in *Egypt* enabled us to reach *Har Sinai* and receive the *Torah*. Only a nation that endured suffering could truly recognize *Hashem's chesed* and accept His covenant. In that journey, the faith of the women, quiet, steadfast, and hopeful, brought salvation to the nation.

Kriat Yam Suf teaches us that the sea does not always split first.

Miriam teaches us what to do while waiting: pick up a tambourine and trust G-d.

This year, *Parashat Beshalach*, *Shabbos Shira*, falls right before *Tu B'Shvat*.

There is a beautiful connection between *Shabbos Shirah* and *Tu B'Shvat*, the New Year for Trees.

A tree grows quietly and patiently, often unseen for years before its fruits appear, much like faith. *Shabbos Shirah* reminds us of the moment when hidden belief bursts into song, while *Tu B'Shvat* teaches us to honor the slow, faithful growth that precedes revelation.

Just as *Miriam* prepared tambourines long before redemption, a tree prepares its fruit deep within the soil long before it is visible. Both teach us that spiritual growth does not happen in an instant; it is nurtured through trust, perseverance, and roots anchored deeply in *emuna*.

When we bless the fruits on *Tu B'Shvat*, we affirm our belief that what *Hashem* plants, within the earth and within our souls, will ultimately blossom into blessing, redemption, and song. All we need to do is trust.

May we merit to transform bitterness into song, silence into faith, and to sing again, soon, with *Moshe* and *Miriam* at the final redemption, *bimhaira b'yameinu*.

Keren Miller is an *emuna* life coach, motivational speaker, and educator with over 25 years of experience. She directs *Lev HaAm*, fostering unity and *Ahavat Yisrael*, and teaches women worldwide *emuna, tefila, and hashkafa*. She is available for private coaching and speaking engagements and offers a free 40-minute consultation.

▶ **Living Inspired with Keren Miller**
◉ **Group & Status: Living Inspired** (private message to join)
✉ **kmillercoaching@gmail.com**

WHAT PURIM ASKS OF US

BY REBBETZIN TZIPORAH HELLER GOTTLIEB

"ESTHER HA MALKA" / BY SHEVA CHAYA / SHEVACHAYA.COM

WHEN GIVING BECOMES ABOUT US

Among the four *mitzvot* of *Purim*, there is one whose deeper significance is very often overlooked: *Mishloach Manot*.

Very often, because we are people, the gift becomes self-oriented. Does it look good? Will they like it? Does it have a nice theme? Will they be impressed? But that is not what *Mishloach Manot* is supposed to be. It is meant to be as though you are sending a portion of your own meal. You want their company. You

want to eat with them. You like them. It is about them, not about you.

Unfortunately, *Mishloach Manot* often turns into something elaborate and competitive. It has to look a certain way, it has to be numerous, it has to be impressive. And in that process, we forget something very important that the *Rambam* teaches. He says that whatever you spend on *Mishloach Manot* should be less than what you spend on *Matanot La'Evyonim*.

Hashem loves when you give to the poor. They are the ones in need. They are the ones who experience real joy from your gift. That is where the emphasis should be. With *Mishloach Manot*, the *avodah* is to see the other person in a bigger light and ourselves in a more dimmed light. With *Matanot La'Evyonim*, there is a unique joy in saying, "I made his day."

I want to tell you a true story. We have friends, the Stillmans, this is their real name. One *Purim*, they came to us with *Mishloach Manot*, arriving by taxi. By that point, the husband was already quite drunk. He asked the driver how much the ride cost. The driver said sixty shekels. The husband replied, "I'm not giving you sixty. I'm giving you one hundred and sixty, but in dollars."

I am not sure the numbers are exact, but it was something like that. He made the driver's day. That is *Purim*. That is the spirit of *Purim*. Not worrying whether the red matches the plate.

LEARNING TO SEE BEYOND NATURE

Purim is known as the holiday of hidden miracles. One of the most hidden aspects of the *Megillah* is something we often forget: the people living the story could not see it the way we do.

We read the *Megillah* and everything is revealed to us. But imagine living in one of the one hundred and twenty-seven provinces of *Achashverosh*. You hear about the decree. The antisemitism was far worse than anything you could have imagined in your worst nightmares. And then, suddenly, everything turns upside down. *Mordechai* becomes important. The Jews are rejoicing. It is clear that this did not happen through natural means.

Recognizing *Hashem* orchestrating events requires a willingness to see, not only with your eyes.

PHOTO: COURTESY OF REBBETZIN TZIPORAH HELLER GOTTLIEB

Bring this into our own times. Any normal human being, without needing to be especially spiritual or especially intelligent, can look at world history and say that Israel should not exist. We are small. We are surrounded by enemies. We do not have a history of being militarily gifted.

WHEN EVERYTHING WENT WRONG

We experienced October 7th, when everything that could go wrong did go wrong. Warnings were missed. Phone calls were not answered. Emails were sent instead of action. Soldiers were mobilized far too late.

And yet, there was salvation. A miraculous salvation. Anyone who wants to see it as a miracle can see it. Even those who cannot open their eyes fully do not believe it was the military alone. They say "somehow." But that somehow is *Hashgacha*. That somehow is *Hashem*.

The danger is apathy. I remember the day the hostages were released. I thought it was a day I would never forget. And now, I wake up in the morning thinking about breakfast. We get used to miracles.

THE VOICE OF DOUBT

Every character in the *Purim* story teaches us something. Even *Haman*.

The *Gemara* asks: where is *Haman* hinted to in the *Torah*? In the words spoken by the snake in *Gan Eden*: *HaMin ha'etz*, "Did you eat from the tree?"

The *Satan* has a function. If you turn the word into a verb, it means to introduce doubt. But the *Satan* does not introduce himself openly. He does not say, "Hello, I am the *Satan*." He sounds like you. What if? What if this is too hard? What if you cannot manage?

Those voices are dangerous because we do not identify them as the *Satan*.

Here is an example. In America, decades ago, getting a *Shomer Shabbat* job was extremely difficult. Friends of mine, from a very committed family, made a decision when they married: no matter what, they would keep *Shabbat*. The question came immediately: What if you do not find a job? What will you do then?

The answer is: not to answer.

Do not explain. Do not justify. Just do.

The husband worked in the post office, far below his abilities, because it allowed him to keep *Shabbat*. That was his answer. He is no longer alive, but he was one of the truly great people of his generation.

You must learn not to answer everything. Otherwise, you allow someone else to write your script.

TWO READINGS, TWO ROLES

We read the *Megillah* twice for a reason.

The night reading is about danger and fear. It is darkness. Put yourself in the story. Be *Mordechai*. You warned them not to go to the feast, and they did not listen. *Haman* is empowered, and you do not know how you will survive.

The day reading is different. During the day, be *Esther*.

Esther was an orphan. She was chosen for her beauty. She was trapped in a palace she never wanted to be in. And yet, no one in Jewish history saved the Jewish people the way *Esther* did. She alone was responsible for the physical salvation of the entire nation.

When you hear the *Megillah* during the day, see the *Esther* in yourself. You can do what nobody else can do.

What makes people happy is love and achievement. We want to love, and we want to achieve.

Love people more. Identify with them. Give to them. You will be happy when they are happy.And achievement comes from recognizing your *tafkid*. When life asks more of you than you expected, see that challenge as exactly what you were meant for.

That is what *Purim* asks of us.

May you have a joyful and meaningful *Purim*, filled with real connection, generosity, and clarity.
May you learn to see the miracles that surround you, even when they are hidden.
May you have the strength to do what is right without needing to justify yourself, and the courage to step into the role only you can fill.

Rebbetzin Tziporah Heller Gottlieb is a renowned *Torah* educator, lecturer, and author, known for her depth, clarity, and insight into Jewish thought. She teaches women worldwide, illuminating *Chumash*, *hashkafa*, and the inner life of *mitzvot* with wisdom, warmth, and intellectual rigor.

🌐 TziporahHellerGottlieb.com
✉ tziporahheller.contact@gmail.com

Let Him: Discovering Hashem in the Hidden Moments

BY REBBETZIN CHANA WEISBERG

PHOTO: COURTESY OF REBBETZIN CHANA WEISBERG

Everywhere today, people are talking about the "Let Them" theory, a modern empowerment idea made popular by Mel Robbins. The concept is surprisingly simple. If someone does something to you, let them. Let them think what they think. Let them behave how they behave. Don't internalize it. Don't let their choices control your peace. Just let them.

People resonate so deeply with those two words that they've even tattooed them on their bodies. Let them. Two words that create emotional space, freedom, and release.

But as I was learning about *Purim*, it struck me that for us, the Jewish people, the real phrase is not "Let Them," but "Let Him."

So much of what happens in our world is beyond our control. So much feels dark, confusing, and upside down. And yet the story of *Purim* reminds us that *Hashem* is behind everything, even when He is hidden, even when nothing makes sense. If we could shift from "let them" to "let Him," let *Hashem* run the world, let

Hashem guide the process, let Hashem reveal the purpose in the end, we would feel that same release, but on a far deeper level.

After all, Megillat Esther is the only sefer in Tanach in which Hashem's name does not appear even once. The entire story is wrapped in hiddenness, hester panim. Even Esther's name comes from hester, hiddenness. And yet, behind the scenes, Hashem is orchestrating every detail.

That is why the story of Purim feels so relevant today. We believed that in a modern, enlightened world, antisemitism could not return. And yet, here it is again, raw and relentless. In the Megillah, it begins with one man, Haman, whose ego is threatened by a single Jew, Mordechai, who refuses to bow. One Jew who will not surrender his essence is enough to enrage him into wanting to destroy an entire nation.

Haman understood something terrifyingly true. If there is one Mordechai, then there is a people who will never truly bow, who will never fully blend in, who carry something unbreakable inside them.

Ironically Hitler y'sh in the most twisted way, understood this. He said that even if a single Jewish child survived without Torah, without education, without a synagogue, Judaism would still live in his soul. He grasped what our own teachers have always taught. The Jewish soul carries an innate G-dliness that cannot be erased.

That is why antisemitism is irrational. Jews are hated when they are rich and when they are poor, when they

assimilate and when they remain observant. It is not about behavior. It is about essence. The Jewish soul carries a Divine frequency, and evil senses it. It is allergic to holiness.

This is why our enemies target not only leaders, but children. We saw it on October 7th. We saw it when hostages were told, "Convert and we will treat you better." The same choice Jews faced in Persia was presented again. Abandon your identity, and you may survive.

And yet, not one Jew converted. Not in Shushan. Not in Gaza.

The Megillah tells us that during the entire year between the decree and the appointed day of destruction, not one Jew said, "I don't need Judaism." Under unbearable pressure, their essence emerged. And today we witness the same reality. Jewish students on hostile campuses declare, "This is who I am." Hostages keeping Shabbat in tunnels by flashlight. People who hadn't prayed in years begging for a siddur or pair of tzitzit. Chanukah menorah lightings that attract huge crowds, just days after the Bondi massacre. When the Jew is squeezed to the limit, the kishkes, the deepest inner truth, comes out.

This is V'nahafoch Hu. When darkness tightens its grip, essence emerges.

There is a turning point in the Megillah. "Ba-layla ha-hu," on that night, the king cannot sleep. Since Hashem's name is hidden throughout the Megillah, Chazal teach that "the King" also refers to the King of the Universe. It is night, a time of concealment, even double darkness.

And precisely then, the Jewish people's inner awakening awakens heavenly mercy. When our essence rises, *Hashem* reciprocates and "awakens," so to speak.

This is the profound contrast between Sinai and *Purim*. At Sinai, there was open revelation. Miracles. Clarity. We said *Na'aseh V'Nishma*, but the choice was overwhelming. How could we say no?

Purim was different. No miracles. No revelation. The Temple destroyed. Prophecy gone. Darkness everywhere. And yet, the Jews "accepted what they had already accepted." This time, not because it was obvious, but because it was who they were. It was the essence of their being. They chose *Hashem* in the dark.

That is why the *mitzvot* of *Purim* reflect desire rather than obligation. On *Purim*, we do not wait for a poor person to come to us; we seek them out. We do not give gifts only in response; we initiate connection. We act not just out of duty, but out of identity.

And so, this *Purim*, as we live through our own *hester panim*, the invitation is simple.

Let Him.
Let *Hashem* guide the story.
Let *Hashem* reveal the hidden light.

We are still here. Thousands of years after Sinai. Thousands of years after Shushan. Still choosing. Still shining.

May this *Purim* bring "*ohr, simcha, sasson vikar*" to all of *Am Yisrael* and to the world. May we merit to see with our eyes what our souls already know. *Hashem* is here, even in the hiddenness, and the greatest miracles begin in the darkest night.

Rebbetzin Chana Weisberg is host of the Ordinary People, Extraordinary Stories podcast and curator of advanced learning experiences on Chabad.org. She is a sought-after speaker and writer. She teaches *Torah* with depth and warmth, focusing on relationships, faith, emotional well-being, and Jewish womanhood, inspiring women worldwide through practical wisdom and spiritual insight.

🌐 chanaweisberg.com
✉ chanaw@gmail.com

PURIM, SIMPLICITY, AND JOY:
A TEACHING FROM THE BAAL SHEM TOV

ART "AYIN TOVA" / BY SHEVA CHAYA / SHEVACHAYA.COM

BY CHANA JENNY WEISBERG

Purim is almost here, and many of us are already busy with costumes, *Mishloach Manot*, menu planning, and the dozens of details that somehow sneak onto our to-do lists every year. As I was preparing myself mentally for the coming rush, my husband shared a story about the *Baal Shem Tov* that struck me as the perfect reminder for this season.

THE BAAL SHEM TOV AND THE TOBACCO

In the 17th century, tobacco came in two types: one that was completely kosher and another that contained additives that made its *kashrut* questionable. Since tobacco is smoked, not eaten, using the questionable one was not halachically forbidden. Still, the *Baal Shem Tov* chose the extra stringency of smoking only the kosher type.

One day, someone gave him tobacco, and after he smoked it, he realized it was the questionable kind. He was crushed. He fell into sadness, upset with himself for having slipped from the stringency he had taken upon himself.

But after sitting with this for a while, he came to a powerful realization.

By allowing a stringency to make him miserable, he was neglecting a far more fundamental *mitzvah*: serving *Hashem* with joy.

His great-grandson, *Rebbe Nachman*, later expressed this beautifully:
"Mitzvah Gedolah Lihyot B'simcha Tamid."
It is a great *mitzvah* to always be joyful.

That became the *Baal Shem Tov's* turning point. He understood that a voluntary *chumra* had overshadowed a core Torah value.

PURIM: THE BASIC MITZVOT ARE SIMPLE

As I reflected on this story, I looked up the basic halachic requirements of *Purim* (from Chabad.org). They are wonderfully simple:

- Hear the *Megillah* once at night and once during the day.
- Give *Mishloach Manot* to one person, consisting of two food items. A cake and a drink are enough.
- Give *Matanot La'Evyonim*, gifts of money or food, to at least two poor people.
- Have a *Purim seudah*, a festive meal during the day.

That is it. That is the *mitzvah*.

Everything else we pile on top, matching themed *Mishloach Manot* for twenty families, homemade gourmet *hamantaschen*, elaborate costumes for kids who cannot even say *"Purim,"* color-coordinated tablescapes, are optional.

Optional can be fun and meaningful. Optional can also become overwhelming and draining.

And that is where the Baal Shem Tov's message becomes so relevant.

WHEN OUR EXTRAS BECOME CHUMROT WE DID NOT CHOOSE

Some people genuinely thrive on creativity. I once knew a woman in my old neighborhood who was a fashion designer for the Israeli brand *Tamnoon*. *Purim*, for her, was an art exhibition. Her children's costumes were breathtaking works of velvet and embroidery. Her *sukkah* looked like a museum installation. The extra effort filled her with joy.

But most of us are not fashion designers. And many of us are not in a phase of life where elaborate creativity brings us calm.

Yet we can fall into the mindset of:

"I did twenty *Mishloach Manot* last year, so I cannot do fewer this year."

"All the other moms are sending themed packages."

"My toddler needs a perfect costume for the photos."

"The *seudah* has to include three appetizers, two meats, and homemade desserts."

Suddenly, the add-ons turn into a burden.

We get tired.
We get impatient.
We get snappy with our kids and husbands.

The joy drains away, exactly what *Purim* is meant to increase.

Purim is about *nafoch hu*, turning things upside down. But for many mothers, the upside-down feeling comes from pressure, not laughter. From exhaustion, not celebration. And often, the pressure does not come from *halacha*. It comes from expectations we internalized without noticing.

Just like the *Baal Shem Tov* with his tobacco, we have to ask ourselves:

Are our self-imposed stringencies helping us serve *Hashem*, or are they pulling us away from joy?

A SIMPLE QUESTION FOR PURIM PREPARATION

As we enter these final days before *Purim*, here is a question worth asking before every task, recipe, costume, or shopping trip:

- Will this bring more joy into my home, or less?
- Will it make me calmer or more stressed?
- More present or more overwhelmed?
- More joyful or more resentful?

Because joy is not just a nice feeling. It is a *mitzvah*.

And not just any mitzvah, but one considered foundational by the *Baal Shem Tov* and all of *Chassidus*.

If an extra task adds beauty, creativity, or bonding, wonderful.
But if it steals your peace, your patience, or your ability to enjoy the day, then it may be time to let it go or scale it back.

Our children will not remember whether the *Mishloach Manot* were Pinterest-perfect. But they will remember how we made the home feel.

They will remember whether *Purim* felt light and happy or tense and rushed.

And the atmosphere of the home is often shaped far more by a mother's emotional state than by the menu or the costumes.

"MIRIAM'S DRUM" BY SHEVA CHAYA / SHEVACHAYA.COM

A BLESSING TO JEWISH MOMS

As we prepare for *Purim*, I want to bless all of us:

May we choose joy over pressure.
May we choose simplicity when simplicity brings peace.
May we choose creativity when creativity brings delight.
May we remember that *Hashem* wants our hearts, our smiles, and our presence far more than themed packaging or elaborate meals.

And may our homes be filled with light, warmth, laughter, and genuine *simcha* this *Purim.*

Wishing all of you a joyful and meaningful *Purim*, dear Jewish moms.

Chana Jenny Weisberg is a writer, speaker, and founder of JewishMOM. com, offering daily inspiration and support for Jewish mothers worldwide. Based in Jerusalem, she writes about faith, parenting, and everyday Jewish life, and is the author of Expecting Miracles and One Baby Step at a Time.

🌐 **JewishMOM.com**
📱 **WhatsApp group:** Email for access
✉️ **chanajennyw@gmail.com**

SPONSORED

POMERANZ
BOOKSELLER

ALWAYS
IN JERUSALEM,
NOW ONLINE!

VISIT US AT: **POMERANZBOOKS.CO.IL**

📍 ADDRESS: BE'ERI 5, JERUSALEM, BETWEEN BETZALEL AND HILLEL
📞 WHATSAPP US: **02-623-5559**

| FRIENDLY STAFF | LARGE VARIETY | WORLDWIDE DELIVERY | NAME ENGRAVING | GIFT CARDS | CONVENIENT LOCATION |

When Women Laugh Together: Finding Simcha Through Connection

ART "ENRAPTURED" BY EVA BIBAS

BY ANNIE ORENSTEIN

"Life is worth living as long as there's a laugh in it."
—Lucy Maud Montgomery

rowing up with my grandparents in New York, I would hear my beloved grandfather laughing from the other side of the house. My grandmother, very early on, would always say, "Laugh at yourself. Don't take yourself too seriously."

Those words follow me everywhere today, as they are truly medicine for my soul.

I had the privilege of getting to know three amazing women who bring light through laughter into women's lives. They take the edge off our fears and worries and help us release the tension inside us. Through laughter, they remind us that we are alive and well, and that we have much to be grateful for.

Let's help each other find the humor in our lives and share it with others. *Purim Sameach.*

DEBBIE HIRSCH

Laughter Yoga, Embodied Joy & Uplifting Women

Debbie shares with our readers about the following topics:

HOW DOES LAUGHTER HELP WOMEN FEEL LESS ALONE?

We are living in a world that is very stressful, and many times we find ourselves alone with our struggles. We can help each other find humor in the things we go through each day.

After a workshop I did a few years ago, a woman came over to me and told me she hadn't laughed in two years, ever since her husband passed away. During the workshop, she laughed, and afterward she said she had forgotten how good it felt to laugh.

What I noticed was a physical shift. Her face softened, her body relaxed, and her energy changed. It wasn't dramatic, but it was real.

I don't think it's about whether the laughter is "real" or intentional. It's the shared experience. Laughter connects people very quickly, without needing explanations. It bypasses words and defenses in a way that talking often can't.

WHAT DO YOU SEE HAPPEN IN A ROOM WHEN WOMEN GIVE THEMSELVES PERMISSION TO PLAY?

When women give themselves permission to try new things and play, they discover so much about themselves that they didn't know.

PHOTO COURTESY OF DEBBIE HIRSCH

The first thing I usually notice is fear. Getting up in front of people and trying something new is scary. You can see it in the body: hesitation, stiffness, and people wanting to disappear into their chairs.

What I tell women is that yes, it's scary to get up, but it's even scarier not to. At 120, *Hashem* won't ask us why we failed. He'll ask us why we didn't use the gifts and talents He gave us.

The release happens when women realize it doesn't matter if they succeed. Showing up is the brave part. The results are in *Hashem's* hands.

HOW CAN SOMEONE ADD MORE SIMCHA AND ENERGY INTO THEIR LIFE?

Simcha isn't a goal. It's something that comes from not being overly critical or overly serious, and from stepping slightly outside your comfort zone.

You can't force *simcha* or chase it. It comes naturally.

When women are disconnected from simcha, it shows up in the body as heaviness and low energy. Play, movement, and laughter help restore energy because they work through the body, not through logic or convincing yourself to feel differently.

Everyone has a different source of what gives them simcha. It can be dance, writing, reading, cooking, baking, and more.

To figure out what gives you simcha, ask yourself, "Does this give me energy? Does it make me want to grow more?"

Simcha and energy go together.

WHAT IS THE INNER CHILD?

The inner child is the part of you that's curious and not afraid to try new things. It doesn't have anxiety about making mistakes. It just wants to play.

For many women, play feels uncomfortable at first because they're used to being responsible, careful, and in control. Letting go can feel unsafe.

What heals is remembering that you're allowed to try, to be imperfect, and to enjoy yourself without needing a reason.

HOW DOES LAUGHTER HELP US RELEASE STRESS?

Life's challenges can feel like either a comedy or a horror movie. You can't be in both at the same time. The body chooses one mode or the other.

Laughter helps shift the body out of stress mode. You can see changes in breathing, grounding, and emotional regulation afterward.

This is especially important for women who are constantly holding it together. Laughter isn't avoidance. It's a reset.

IN YOUR VIEW, HOW IS UPLIFTING EACH OTHER A FORM OF AVODAT HASHEM?

So much of our stress comes from worrying about what others think of us, like on the first day of school or a new job. There is a lot of self-criticism going on in our heads.

The moment we focus on another person, ask their name, offer help, or include them, that self-criticism quiets down. When we lift someone else up, we lift ourselves up too.

That's why uplifting others is such a powerful form of *Avodat Hashem*. It's serving *Hashem* through action, not just thought.

ANY PRACTICAL TIP YOU WOULD LIKE TO SHARE WITH OUR READERS?

"Wrong Answers Only"

Look at any object near you, a pen, a mug, a phone.

Point to it and say out loud, "This is a…" and then give a completely wrong answer.

For example, point to a cup and say, "This is a frog."

Do five to ten wrong answers quickly, switching objects as you go.

This exercise breaks the habit of needing to be correct or perfect. It brings you into the present moment, sparks creativity, opens you up to other possibilities, and reconnects you with spontaneity, without any pressure to feel happy.

A FEW MORE IDEAS TO SUM IT UP:

Simcha isn't a pursuit. It's something that comes naturally. Let go of self-criticism and instead enjoy the freedom of believing in yourself.

Stop being overly serious. It's the number one *simcha* killer. Somehow, our remedy for not playing all the time became a prison where we never play at all.

Step slightly outside your comfort zone, because nothing beats the joy of overcoming a fear or an obstacle.

BAZY RUBIN

Real Life Humor, Miluima Strength & Uplifting Through Honesty

HOW DOES SHARING YOUR REAL LIFE UPLIFT WOMEN GOING THROUGH SIMILAR STRUGGLES?

This might sound crazy, but every single person who goes through something starts out believing they are the only one.

When the war broke out, I thought I must be the only one who was drowning or freaking out about her husband on the front lines and worrying about how to give four little ones a sense of normalcy in a scary world.

Then I started sharing the real parts: the messy kitchen, the emotional roller coasters, the months I'm parenting alone during *miluim*, and the small wins I'm proud of.

Through sharing these reels, I have been able to help people see themselves and realize that they are not alone at all. I'm not giving them a curated version of strength. I'm showing the strength that comes from simply getting up every

PHOTO BY JOSHUA FLEISHER

morning and insisting on finding *simcha* in the chaos of our lives.

When we speak honestly about our struggles, it turns loneliness into connection. Suddenly someone out there feels less crazy, less "not enough," and more like, okay, if she can get through this, maybe I can too.

WHAT ROLE DOES HUMOR PLAY IN JEWISH RESILIENCE?

Humor is our national coping mechanism. It's how we've survived every impossible chapter in our history, by laughing through it, not ignoring it.

For me, humor is the glue that holds the broken pieces until they're ready to be whole again. It allows us to acknowledge the pain without drowning in it.

Jewish humor isn't escapism. It's courage. It's saying, "Yes, this is hard, but we still choose joy, connection, and life." Sometimes a joke is exactly what we need to stay just above water.

WHAT MESSAGE DO YOU WANT EVERY OVERWHELMED MOTHER TO HEAR IN ADAR?

You don't have to show up big. You just have to show up.

משנכנס אדר מרבין בשמחה
"Mishenichnas Adar, Marbin B'Simcha."

Adar is the time when we need to increase joy, not manufacture it. Joy doesn't always look like confetti and costumes. Sometimes joy is letting yourself lower expectations in order to catch a break, letting yourself laugh instead of cry, and letting yourself be imperfect while still feeling worthy.

If you're overwhelmed, you're not failing. You're human.

Hashem doesn't ask you to be a superhero.

WHAT DOES HASHEM WANT OF US?

Hashem asks us to do our best, work with what we've got, and be *b'simcha* as much as we can.

Bazy Rubin is a content creator, video editor, and miluima, a reservist's wife, who uses social media to inspire, encourage, and bring *simcha*. Through humor and authentic storytelling, she shares the emotional reality of life during war, helping women find strength, perspective, and connection in uncertain times, with honesty, warmth, purpose, and human insight.

📷 @bazyrubin

JOAN WEINER
Comedy, Creative Mindset & Uplifting Through Perspective

HOW DOES COMEDY HELP WOMEN BALANCE BUSY LIVES DURING CHALLENGING TIMES?

Jewish women share a specific place in the world that can only really be described properly using comedy.

On the one hand, we are taught that as *Hashem's* last official creation, we are also His holiest creation. In the deepest parts of our *neshamot*, we carry the highest levels of spirituality. As the ones who bring life into the world, we are literal partners in creation. We are essentially more spiritual than physical.

At the same time, as Jewish women, every day we roll up our sleeves and get to work tending to the needs of our medium to large families. Basically, we make Thanksgiving every *Shabbat*, with guests and all.

From one perspective, we are the most spiritual, and at the same time, we are the hardest working people in the world. My comedy talks about this a lot.

Explaining this in a comedic way helps women appreciate the unique place we hold in the world and gives context to our lives. It makes women feel seen.

Comedy helps us see the light during hard times. Laughter comes at the end, when there is a resolution to something that made no sense.

As we say in *benching* every *Shabbat*, in *Shir Hamaalot, "Az Yimaleh Schok Pinu,"* then we will laugh. The laughter we experience now is just a sample of what is to come.

WHAT MAKES HUMOR SUCH A POWERFUL FORM OF EMOTIONAL SUPPORT?

Humor and laughter help people step outside of themselves. When you laugh, even for a moment, you are a different person.

Laughter connects people. It exists in a special, elevated spiritual category. Like food and physical intimacy, laughter is a gift given to the world by *Hashem*.

When used the right way, it connects people. If you laugh with someone, you naturally feel closer to them. You bond with them, just as you do when you share a meal or a meaningful relationship.

PHOTOCREDIT COURTESY OF JOAN WEINER & SURI KATZ

The physical benefits of laughter are well studied and well known. Laughter lowers blood pressure and releases good brain chemicals.

But it is spiritually powerful too. Laughter helps you rise above your situation. Humor has always been one of our most powerful survival mechanisms. When we had no other way to fight back, against Nazis, against antisemitism, and against powerlessness, we have maintained our ability to laugh.

Jews have long been associated with laughter and comedy. It is truly one of our people's strongest survival skills.

If you can laugh at something, you know you can overcome it.

HOW DO YOU USE PERFORMANCE TO HELP WOMEN SHIFT PERSPECTIVE?

It is about using a woman's voice.

I like to hold up a mirror to Jewish women and say, look at your life. Look how incredible you are. Who else can do what you do?

As an olah to Israel, I face the challenges of aliyah by laughing at them, and I do the same with the challenges of parenthood. It's difficult sometimes, but even when I have a difficult day, I tell myself, "Well, at least it's good material."

I want to help all women think of challenges that way. Some days are hard, but if we can laugh at them, we can survive them.

WHAT JEWISH VALUES SHAPE YOUR APPROACH TO UPLIFTING YOUR AUDIENCE?

I believe laughter is holy and is a gift from Hashem, and it has to be used properly. Anything that mocks, demeans, or belittles is not okay.

I would never do insult comedy or a roast. I want my audience to walk away feeling better about their lives and their experiences by seeing themselves in a new light, not by looking down at others.

WHAT DOES IT MEAN TO YOU TO BRING WOMEN JOY IN A DIFFICULT WORLD?

It is truly a gift and a blessing.

When I was younger, I hid behind sarcasm and negative humor as a coping mechanism. Over the years, I have shifted into seeing humor as a gift. When I am on stage, I am offering that gift to the audience.

Laughter belongs to this physical world. If we can laugh, it means we are still here, and we can still do the serious work this world requires of us.

Sometimes we need to give ourselves permission to laugh. The world is in a dark place right now. We have lived through a war, and there are many people who are not ready to laugh again, and that must be respected. But when someone needs a laugh, I am honored to give it, the way you might deliver food or offer a hug. I have a laugh to give.

Joan Weiner is a stand-up comedian and writer who blends sharp humor with Jewish life, motherhood, and modern absurdities. A former winner of The Jewish Week's Funniest Amateur Comedian, she performs internationally and is currently developing a one-woman show exploring faith, family, and the chaos of becoming yourself.

🌐 www.joanweiner.com
✉ jwlevin@gmail.com

Annie Orenstein has been producing shows for women and girls since 2006. In 2010, she co-founded *Spotlight On Women*. She is passionate about producing open mics for performers to grow professionally and for Jewish women to be inspired. She also hosted *Spotlight On Women Radio* and writes in local newspapers and magazines highlighting artists. She lives in Maaleh Adumim with her family.

✉ Annie.spotlight@gmail.com

SPONSORED

SHEVACH! TORAH and THE ARTS WOMEN'S PROGRAM

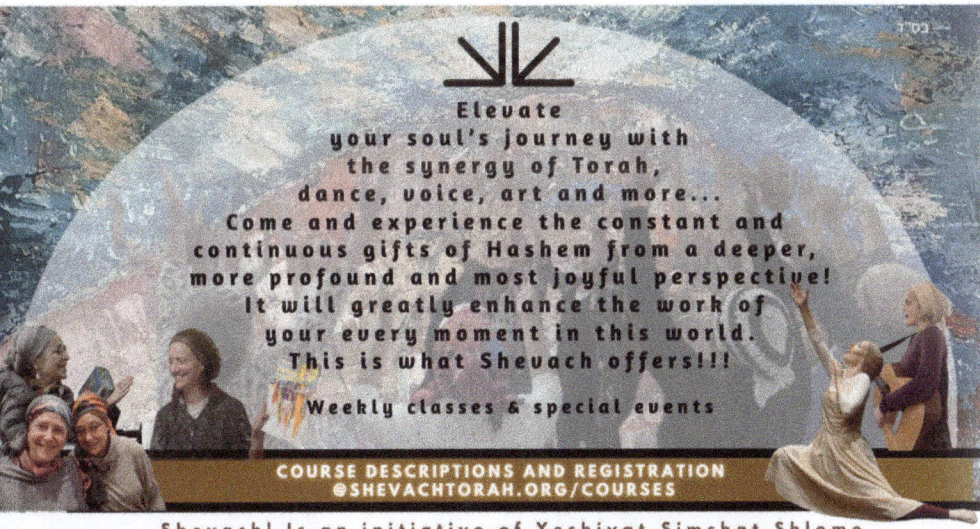

Elevate
your soul's journey with
the synergy of Torah,
dance, voice, art and more...
Come and experience the constant and
continuous gifts of Hashem from a deeper,
more profound and most joyful perspective!
It will greatly enhance the work of
your every moment in this world.
This is what Shevach offers!!!

Weekly classes & special events

COURSE DESCRIPTIONS AND REGISTRATION
@SHEVACHTORAH.ORG/COURSES

Shevach! Is an initiative of Yeshivat Simchat Shlomo

📍 18 HAGILBOA , NACHLAOT
📞 +972-52-939-3302
🌐 shevachtorah@gmail.com

SHEVACH

On Torah, Creativity, Sisterhood, & Inclusivity

TZELOFCHAD" BY LAURA BEN-DAVID Z"L

BY TOBY KLEIN GREENWALD

There are many elements that influence our lives. As a child, I wrote poetry, put on plays, and last but definitely not least, loved learning *Torah*.

Sometimes those intersecting loves demanded difficult decisions. After studying in public school and an afternoon *Talmud Torah*, I switched to a Jewish day school for high school. It meant giving up courses in drama and journalism had I gone to the local public

high school, though I continued my creative efforts in school and *B'nei Akiva* and *Camp Moshava*.

And then I came to Israel. And stayed, beyond a gap year, to study *Torah* at the *Michlala*. It meant not returning to a prestigious university in the US.

These are decisions that define our lives.

I immersed myself in *Torah* learning and teaching, while embedding creative writing and drama in my lessons, filling

In 1996, Dr. Michael Tobin, a psychologist in our town of Efrat, asked me to join him and others to create *WholeFamily.com*, a website whose core was short dramas depicting conflicts in family relationships, with advice from professionals.

When the dot coms crashed in 2000, we morphed our website into a theater troupe, supported by the OU Israel Center and the Jewish Agency. It was a life lesson, not giving up, but going forward in a new way.

We invited the audience on stage to improvise with our actors, seeking solutions. During one scene, when a teen actress was describing her challenge of drug addiction, we could hear gentle crying from parents in the audience. We performed throughout Israel, including before populations suffering from rocket attacks or, later, displacement from Gush Katif. Once again, I saw how theater could alleviate trauma.

notebooks with poetry, working for a publishing company, and eventually receiving degrees in English Literature as well. I turned to journalism and loved writing about inspiring women and inspiring events in our Israeli life. I also wrote investigative pieces and published stories about Nazi war criminals, terror, and other difficult topics.

I discovered the gift and relief that creativity can bring to those who are struggling. The voice urging me to touch other souls came from within, and I believe from *Hashem*.

In 1975, while working for Gesher in Sfat, I also gave a drama course to students who, in 1974, had been in the Maalot terror attack, where 22 of their schoolmates were murdered by terrorists. That was my first experience using drama to help heal deep wounds.

PHOTO: "HEROINES" BY REBECCA KOWALSKY

Around the same time, the second intifada assaulted our lives.

In 2001, a friend of mine, Sharon Katz, inspired by a poster she had of Mickey Rooney and Judy Garland from the film *Strike Up the Band*, which was made following the Great Depression, sent out an email: "We're putting on a play!" I volunteered to direct, Arlene Chertoff choreographed, Sharon produced, a hundred women joined us, and the Raise Your Spirits Summer Stock Company was born. In 2010, we changed our name to Raise Your Spirits Theatre.

We decided not to cancel rehearsals or performances on the day of a terror attack. This was not easy. One young woman lost a close friend in the Sbarro attack. She wanted to leave. After two weeks, I went to her home and told her gently, "You have mourned. Now do it for her. In her memory. In her honor." She came back.

Our second performance fell on September 11th. A local rabbi advised us to perform and to open the evening with *Tehillim*, as we did before every rehearsal. While books of Psalms were gathered for the audience, I spoke to the cast backstage and shared that relatives of mine perished in Theresienstadt, people who may also have been theater performers, who continued creating even during the *Shoah*.

That night, we began the custom of ending every performance with *Ani Maamin* and *Hatikva*. Women who attended told us it was one of the most powerful evenings they had ever experienced.

Throughout our, thus far, 14 biblical productions, we became a multi-generational sisterhood. Women who had endured personal trauma, loss, illness, or hardship found camaraderie and strength. Through the years, some of our young actresses struggled with learning disabilities, ADHD, or social challenges. One girl was deaf, another was on the spectrum, and another had Down syndrome. They were all accepted and blossomed.

We hosted families of terror victims, fallen soldiers, and women in financial distress as our guests in the audience.

In one show, we had a dialogue in which Dena, *Yaakov*'s daughter, and Esther compare their painful experiences of being taken by force, by Shechem and by King Achashverosh. We invited women from a battered wives' shelter to that performance, and I imagined some of them identifying with the difficult stories.

In our current RYS show, *Heroines! Songs & Soliloquies for the Soul*, which I direct, monologues of heroines of Oct. 7 intermingle with songs from our biblical shows, highlighting how our present echoes the faith and heroism of the past. Shayna Levine-Hefetz co-created the show with me, Elisheva Savir is music director, and Tammy Rubin, the head of our amuta, is my co-producer. Our next show will be on Miriam.

Other theater projects I directed with teens at risk helped them cope with feelings of rejection and failure. I also watched as girls uprooted from Gush Katif opened their crying souls in another theater project, flying on stage in a dance scene at the seashore, and my heart soared.

My all-female Playback-dance troupe, *Na'na*, has performed for "regular" audiences and also for women who have suffered war, terror, abuse, and other traumas. In 2024, we performed for the women of the IDF *Chevra Kadisha*, those who received, to their loving care, the victims of Oct. 7. It is a performance we will never forget.

In *Mikva the Musical, Music & Monologues from the Deep*, co-created and co-produced by Myra Guterman and myself, one of our talented actresses is a woman who performs in a wheelchair.

Sensitivity to those who deal with challenges or trauma also figured in my teaching of *Torah*, English, and Creative Writing, beyond the scope of this article.

I believe that *Hashem* placed me in particular places at particular times to reach out to someone who needed it.

In 2016, I was hit with breast cancer. I continued to write and to direct, and I felt all the love I had given my casts through the years come flooding back to me. *B'H*, I am fine now.

In closing, I remember sitting *shiva* in Cleveland for my mother during *Purim*, in March 2003. I returned to our last RYS performance of *Esther & the Secrets in the King's Court*. Halachically, I could be there. I was needed in the tech booth. As I came down and waited backstage to join the cast only for a final bow, I thought about how my parents had allowed me to switch schools to learn

more *Torah*. My mother had always been *shomeret Shabbat*. My father, though he became *Torah*-observant only later in life, had agreed as well. Because they saw that *Torah* meant so much to me. And because they were extraordinary people.

And here I was, decades later, listening to a *Torah* musical I had co-authored and directed, and I thought to myself, "Thanks, Mom and Dad. In the end, I have it all."

Follow the voice *Hashem* instills in your hearts, and you too will be able to say: *Hodu l'Hashem ki tov.*

Toby Klein Greenwald is a poet, photographer, journalist, playwright and theater director, and has taught *Torah*, Jewish Thought, English, and Creative Writing. She directs *Raise Your Spirits Theatre*, the *Na'na* and *Hamra Playback* troupes, *Mikva the Musical,* and gives workshops in *BiblioPlayback*. Her work has received awards in both theater and journalism.

🌐 RaiseYourSpirits.org
🌐 PlaybackNana.com
🌐 MikvatheMusical.com
🌐 WholeFamily.com
✉ toby@wholefamily.com

FIRE, ESSENCE, AND THE DIVINE FEMININE IN ART

with Sheva Chaya Shaiman & Eva Bibas

HER TRIBE MAGAZINE

SHEVA CHAYA

A Conversation on Fire, Faith, and Creation

"Just as glass becomes unbreakable through fire, so do we."

Living and creating in Tzfat, Sheva Chaya's work emerges from fire, faith, and deep *kavannah*. Through glass and paint, she transforms fragility into strength, and art into *Avodat Hashem*. This conversation explores creation as prayer, fire as transformation, and beauty as responsibility.

Your work feels deeply spiritual, not just artistic. Can you take us back to the moment you realized that art wasn't just something you do, but something you were called to express?

When I first came to *Eretz Yisrael*, I realized that art should have purpose. I felt it could convey important messages and truths in a unique way. It became clear to me that the subject matter needed to be *Am Yisrael* and *Eretz Yisrael*, something much bigger and more collective than just my personal story.

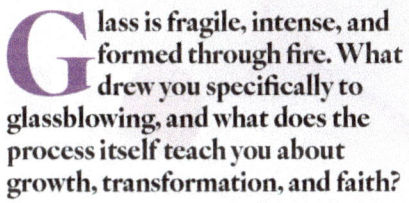

PEACE WILL COME WHEN the ARABS WILL LOVE THEIR CHILDREN MORE THAN THEY HATE US. WE HATE WAR. WE DO NOT REJOICE IN VICTORIES. WE REJOICE WHEN A NEW KIND OF COTTON IS GROWN and WHEN STRAWBERRIES BLOOM IN ISRAEL... THOSE WHO don't know how to WEEP WITH THEIR WHOLE HEART, don't know HOW to LAUGH EITHER... ~GOLDA MEIR

"GOLDA" / ART BY SHEVA CHAYA

Glass is fragile, intense, and formed through fire. What drew you specifically to glassblowing, and what does the process itself teach you about growth, transformation, and faith?

The light and fire drew me to glassblowing. The ability to form a material that is glowing and flowing was, and still is, endlessly interesting. I saw early on that fire transforms glass into the opposite of what we usually think of. Everyone knows how fragile and breakable glass is, because we experience breaking glass regularly in life.

But seeing glass glow, flow, and be blown into interesting and useful forms tells a different story. I began searching for glass in our spiritual sources and came to understand that its very nature teaches us something about ourselves and about transformation.

Just as glass is fragile and breakable, so are we. Yet when glass is heated by fire, it becomes glowing, flowing, and unbreakable. We, too, become unbreakable through our fire. What is our fire? The heart of a Jew, the soul, prayer, a mitzvah, *kavannah*, and many expressions of a life guided by *Torah*. All of these are forms of fire that make the Jewish people unbreakable. They literally bring broken pieces together into a new, beautiful, flowing form.

Fire can destroy, but it can also create something breathtaking. Have there been moments where difficulty or brokenness became a catalyst for deeper creativity or clarity?

Definitely.

101

KIDDUSH CUPS BY SHEVA CHAYA

The darkness of the night is one of the most fertile grounds for creativity. Much of my art has come from inspiration found in very deep, dark places. Creating is a way to find light there.

If you were to describe your art as a form of *Avodat Hashem*, what does that service look like, and how do you hope it impacts *Am Yisrael*?

I think of my art as prayer. With every piece I make, with every brushstroke, there is an opportunity for *kavannah*. I pray for individuals, for the soldiers, the hostages, the families, and for the *achdut* of all of *Am Yisrael*.

I hope my work helps us see our beauty and our strength, and that we recognize

ourselves as a people who bring light into the world.

What is your personal message to our readers enjoying your beautiful art on the back cover of this edition?

"*Miriam's Dream*" reflects the movement in circle form toward harmony, unity, and collective movement in faith and joy which brings us into *geula* consciousness. This movement actually started thousands of years ago who *Miriam* led the women in the circle dance and song after *Am Yisrael* crossed the sea. It is a dreamy vision of the potential we (always) have to unify, and lift up our personal hopes, dreams and prayers to the collective level. This is a taste of *geula* consciousness where the closeness to each other and the Creator are both involved. We are all able to dance as individuals, bringing our uniqueness into expression, while dancing with each other, creating unity, and all the time recognizing that *Hashem*, the Creator of it all, is right in the middle of our collective circle of expression, equally close to each of us as individuals and all of us together.

Looking forward, what are you currently creating, dreaming, or praying into existence, both as an artist and as a woman on her spiritual path?

I hope to find ways to share my art more in Jerusalem and worldwide, to publish more books that combine paintings and writings, and to offer meaningful workshops that bring together art, music, movement, and space. I have a special place in my heart to speak to and reach the children of this generation (and the inner child in all ages) with my work.

I hope my learning becomes useful and inspiring teaching, both conceptually and visually, helping to reveal the greatness of *Am Yisrael* and *Eretz Yisrael*.

I hope my work reaches those it is meant to reach and brings joy, light, and healing to individuals, to *Am Yisrael*, and to the world.

Sheva Chaya Shaiman

Originally from Denver, Sheva Chaya made Aliyah in 1999 and moved to Tzfat in 2005. That same year, she began learning glassblowing, which has since become her passion. Ever since, the land, the people, and the rich

SHEVA CHAYA
THE GLASS BLOWER
OF TZFAT

tradition of spiritual teachings have infused her work with greater depth-work she shares from her gallery in Tzfat and with audiences worldwide. This edition of the magazine prominently features her artwork.

🌐 shevachaya.com
✉ 7alive@gmail.com
📷 @shevachaya

EVA BIBAS
When the *Neshama* Speaks Through Form

"Essence desires to be revealed. Withholding it is a disservice to the whole."

Where Sheva Chaya works with fire and glass, Eva Bibas works with layers, symbols, and inner movement. Her art explores the unseen forces that shape form, meaning, and identity through a deeply *Kabbalistic* lens.

When you create, what part of your *neshama* is asking to be expressed, and what has your artistic journey taught you about trusting your inner voice?

When I create, I aim to express something deeper than my *neshama*, to transmit essence. Just as the Infinite breathed Its essence into *Adam*, I feel a longing for my life force to be revealed through what I make.

This impulse moves through my *koach ha-medameh*, the imaginative faculty that allows the unseen to take form. Shaped by experience and emotion, each work carries my personal imprint while reaching toward the Divine.

My journey has taught me that essence longs to be revealed. When it is withheld, it becomes blocked. Trusting my inner voice means allowing that energy to move, take shape, and be shared.

ART "BURST OF LFE" BY EVA BIBAS

ART "POERTO AZUL" BY EVA BIBAS

If your art had a quiet message it was whispering to the world right now, what would it be?

My work is rooted in the concept of *yichudim*, the unification of opposites. I explore harmony within contradiction through the balance of light and shadow, movement and stillness, growth and wholeness.

An image only takes shape when light and shadow coexist. Darkness is not a failure of light, but the condition that gives it depth and clarity. My work invites viewers to hold complexity, navigate change, and trust the underlying coherence of life.

For a woman who feels disconnected from her creativity, what gentle first step would you invite her to take, especially in the month of Adar, the month of *simcha*?

Kabbalah teaches that women are rooted in the *sefirah* of *bina*, which can draw us into details and perfectionism that block expression. A powerful first step in reconnecting with creativity is shifting focus from outcome to process, allowing the hand or body to move without expectation. Awakening the inner child creates space for curiosity and play. The *simcha* of Adar naturally opens a person to *ruach ha-kodesh*, inviting deeper inspiration and insight.

Creativity can begin simply. Drawing with pencils, pens, crayons, or chalk pastels and letting marks appear freely, creating a moodboard with images, colors, or textures, or painting on a surface that already holds marks using watercolor, gouache, or acrylics allows intuition to lead rather than planning a final result.

Often, self judgment shuts down our freedom to create. These practices invite playfulness, curiosity, and a renewed connection to one's creative spirit.

Purim teaches us that what is most powerful is often hidden. How does your Jewish heritage quietly guide your artistic expression?

Jewish spiritual tradition guides my practice through symbols, materials, and visual language. Hebrew letters, considered the building blocks of creation, appear within my work whether consciously perceived or not.

I also explore the histories of being a Jewish woman in exile, and the resilience and beauty that emerge through memory, movement, and adaptation. Each piece carries hidden threads connecting history, place, and identity.

How has your spiritual journey impacted the layers and intention within your art?

My practice is rooted in intentionality. Every material, gesture, and symbol carries meaning. The layers in my work echo *tzimtzum*, the Divine contraction through which creation emerges, as well as the feminine force that brings life into being.

Over time, I began dedicating each studio session *l'shem shamayim*. With continued learning, deeper meanings reveal themselves, reflecting the endurance of *Torah* through exile and the ongoing refinement of the self.

Starting with a blank canvas and a mission to unite Jewish women before *Mashiach*, how would your creative process begin?

I would begin collaboratively on an irregularly shaped canvas, using multiple media to reflect many voices becoming one. The process would start with presence and alignment through meditation or embodied practice, followed by intuitive collective creation.

The work would embody unity and express the Divine feminine through shared intention and action.

Eva Bibas is a Venezuelan American Jewish interdisciplinary artist whose work explores Kabbalistic thought, transformation, and spirituality. Her work has been exhibited at the Dalí, Pérez, and Rubell Museums and is held in private collections. Her work adds another layer of depth to the pages of this edition.

🌐 evabibasartist.wix.com/home
📷 @ArtisticJewishSoul

SIMPLE ELEGANCE FOR PURIM:

Three Dishes Everyone Loves

BY MENUCHAH ARMEL

As *Purim* approaches, our kitchens fill with laughter, color, and inviting aromas that bring family and friends together. We are sharing three crowd pleasing recipes to enhance your Purim table, perfect between *mishloach manot*, after the *megillah*, or at the festive meal.

Enjoy warm Garlic Twists, colorful Fancy Rice, and Chicken in Sweet and Sour Sauce, a comforting and celebratory main.

May your Purim be filled with joy, good food, and sweet memories,

With Love, Menuchah

PHOTOGRAPHY & FOOD DESIGN: MIRIT HATAV

פורים שמח

Garlic Twists

Yield: 14 twists

The first time I tasted this bread it made such an impression on me that I had to get the recipe. You can make them for a *melave malka* or as an appetizer for a dairy meal. This melt-in-your mouth bread goes well with cream cheese and/or dips.

Dough

4 cups warm water

2 Tbsp. instant dry yeast

1 cup sugar

4 ½ lb. (2 kg) flour

2 Tbsp. salt

1 cup oil

Garlic Topping

¼ cup olive oil

6–8 garlic cloves, minced

1 Tbsp. dried parsley flakes

Dash of salt (optional)

Instructions

1. In a medium bowl, dissolve yeast in water.

2. Add sugar and stir.

3. Add remaining ingredients and mix together by hand.

4. Knead dough until soft and no longer sticky. Add additional flour (if needed).

5. Cover and let rise for 1–2 hours.

6. Take *challah* (with a *bracha*, if required)

7. Preheat the oven to 350° F (180° C)

8. Divide dough into balls. Roll each ball into a 3-inch (7cm) strand, then twist two strands together and pinch lightly at ends.

9. Bake for 30 minutes or until lightly browned.

10. In a large mixing bowl, combine ingredients for Garlic Topping.

11. While still warm, drop twists into Garlic Topping and toss lightly.

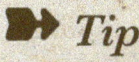 *Tip*

This dough can be shaped as desired. I make twists because they present well in a basket or individually placed beside settings.

Chicken in Sweet & Sour Sesame Sauce

Yield: 10 servings

This recipe is a little fancier than your regular breaded chicken cutlets. I like to make it for extra special occasions.

Breaded Chicken

1 cup flour

½ tsp. salt

Dash of garlic powder

Dash of paprika

2 eggs

3 Tbsp. oil

½ cup water

10 chicken cutlets

Sweet and Sour Sauce

1 cup ketchup

1 cup mayonnaise

4 Tbsp. apricot jam

½ cup honey

2 Tbsp. lemon juice

1 onion, finely diced

½ cup sesame seeds

Instructions

1. Line a 10" × 15" (25 × 38 cm) pan with baking paper.

2. For the Breaded Chicken, in a medium-sized mixing bowl, combine flour, spices, eggs, oil, and water to form a smooth paste.

3. Dip each cutlet in the paste.

4. Fry cutlets in a lightly greased frying pan, for approximately 5 minutes on each side.

5. Arrange cutlets in a single layer in the pan.

6. Preheat the oven to 375° F (190° C).

7. Combine Sweet and Sour Sauce ingredients in a small mixing bowl and stir until smooth.

8. Pour sauce over chicken cutlets and cover tightly with aluminum foil.

9. Bake for 30 minutes.

 *Tip*

If the sauce is too runny, uncover chicken and bake for 10-15 more minutes.

Fancy Rice

Yield: 4 servings | Gluten free

Add a little flair to your table with this recipe. It is an easy way to dress-up rice.

Instructions

1 Tbsp. oil

1 red pepper, diced

1 yellow pepper, diced

4 carrots, shredded

5 cloves garlic, minced

1 cup jasmine rice

1 tsp. salt

2 cups boiling water

Instructions

1. Heat oil in a frying pan.

2. Saute peppers, carrots, and garlic until soft.

3. Add rice and salt, and stir.

4. Add boiling water, stir, and bring to a boil again.

5. Reduce heat, cover, and let simmer for 20 minutes.

6. Turn off heat and let stand, covered, for 10 minutes.

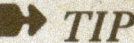 **TIP**

The secret to perfectly fluffy rice is making sure that the water is at a full boil when you add it. I boil the water while I saute the vegetables.

Menuchah Armel Born in Baltimore, MD, and living in Israel since 1995, she turned a love of home cooking into *Menuchah L'simcha Catering.* Cooking for events, *yeshivas*, and seminaries inspired her cookbook *Straight to the Plate.* She teaches simple, delicious cooking with everyday pantry ingredients, sharing calm and practical kitchen skills through workshops and demonstrations.

🌐 straighttotheplate.net

✉ info@straighttotheplate.net

Mishloach Manot

SPICE, SWEETNESS & TRADITION

BY THE SEPHARDIC SPICE GIRLS

Gathering family and friends around the *Shabbat* table or celebrating the Jewish holidays with delicious food is one of the greatest joys in life; it creates lifelong memories and inspires the next generation.

For this *Purim* issue, we are thrilled to share our treasured recipes for traditional Sephardic baked delicacies. Our grandmothers, along with generations of Sephardic women, lovingly prepared these recipes for *Mishloach Manot*, gifting them to friends and family

OJOS DE HAMAN – NORTH AFRICAN PURIM BREAD

A North African tradition handed down many generations.

"Every *Purim*, I make these and reminisce about my childhood and my very special mother, who baked them for us each year," Rachel says.

Ingredients

Challah dough (use your favorite challah recipe)
Eggs (for boiling and for egg wash)
Fennel seeds or sesame seeds (for topping)

Instructions:

Make individual rolls or larger loaves, placing one or more eggs on top.

Boil the eggs, discard the water, and set aside to cool and dry.

Dough:

Use your favorite *challah* recipe.

Beat an egg and use it as glue for the strips of dough that will go on top of the eggs. Set aside.

Punch down the dough, divide it, and separate into equal balls (about 1/3 cup each).

Take one ball, flatten it, and cut it into strips of dough that will hold down the eggs. Set aside.

Take another ball of dough, pierce a hole in the center with your fingers as if making a donut, place an egg in the center, and set on a baking sheet.

Take two strips of dough and form an X over the egg. Use the beaten egg as glue to secure the strips. If they begin to slide, use toothpicks.

Brush the entire top with egg wash.

Sprinkle with fennel seeds or sesame seeds.

Bake until golden.

BA'BA TAMAR

Sharon's grandmother, Nana Aziza, made the most incomparable, delectably tasty *ba'ba tamar*—a classic of the Babylonian kitchen. These thin, four-inch round cookies are made with a crispy, unsweetened dough and a soft, chewy date filling.

DATE FILLING

Ingredients

2 cups date paste
¼ cup olive oil
3 Tbsp water
¼ cup crushed walnuts

Instructions

Combine the dates and olive oil.
Add the water and walnuts and mix until the mixture becomes a smooth paste.
Set aside.
Garnish

Ingredients

3 eggs
1 Tbsp honey
1 Tbsp water
½ cup sesame seeds

Instructions

In a small bowl, beat together the eggs, honey, and water.
Set aside.

DOUGH RECIPE

Ingredients

2 packets active dry yeast
1 tsp sugar
1 tsp kosher salt
2 cups warm water, divided
7 cups all-purpose flour, sifted
1 cup avocado or vegetable oil
1 tsp fennel or nigella seeds

Instructions

In a small bowl, add warm water to the yeast, sugar, and salt. Cover and leave to proof for 10-15 minutes.

In a stand mixer, add the flour, oil, water, fennel seeds, and yeast mixture. Mix until a dough is formed.

Remove the dough from the mixer bowl and knead by hand until smooth and stretchy.

Place the dough in an oiled bowl, rub a little oil over the top, cover with a kitchen towel, and set aside in a warm spot for 1 hour.

Remove the dough and knead for 2 minutes. Return to the bowl and let stand for 25 minutes.

Preheat the oven to 350°F (180°C). Divide the dough into four pieces.

Grease your hands with oil, pinch the dough into golf-ball-size balls, and roll until smooth. Place the dough balls on a greased baking sheet.

Place a ball of dough into the palm of your hand, make a deep indentation, and place half a tablespoon of date filling inside.

Pinch the dough closed. Using a small rolling pin, roll the ball flat until it is about 4 inches in diameter.

With the end of the rolling pin, make a few indentations in the center of the cookie. Place cookies on a baking sheet.

Brush the cookies with the egg mixture and top with sesame seeds.

Repeat until all the dough and date filling are used.

Bake for 12-15 minutes, until golden and crispy.

SESAME BRITTLE

Vegan and gluten-free, it's the perfect quick treat to add to your holidays.

Rachel's Spanish Moroccan family calls sesame brittle "halwa." As a little girl, she recalls her mother, Rica, making it for all their family celebrations, served with a glass of fresh mint (nana) tea.

Sharon's grandmother called sesame brittle "*sim`isiyi*," and always had a tin of it on hand. She would serve it to her guests on long *Shabbat* afternoons with fresh fruit and a small glass of cardamom tea.

Cooking Notes

When making sesame brittle, make sure to lay out all the utensils and have the ingredients pre-measured. Working with hot sugar means having to work quickly, before it has a chance to harden.

The tricky part is to roll the brittle thin. We recommend using a stone countertop or a Silpat non-stick mat on the bottom and another on top of the syrup. Place the rolling pin on top of the mat, to ensure that it doesn't stick.

Ingredients

2   cups white granulated sugar

1   cup raw sesame seeds

1   cup raw slivered almonds, optional

3   Tbsp hot water

vegetable oil
spray

Directions

Spray the work counter with plenty of vegetable spray. Spray the rolling pin and have it ready to use.

In a pan over medium heat, toast the sesame seeds and almonds until golden, then remove from heat.

In a deep, heavy pot, add the sugar and warm over a low flame. As the sugar slowly melts into a caramel, begin to stir with a wooden spoon. Keep stirring until the caramel is dark and golden and all the sugar has dissolved. If sugar lumps appear, keep stirring until they dissolve.

Add the sesame seeds and almonds all at once and stir vigorously. Quickly pour onto the work counter.

Using a well-oiled rolling pin, start to roll the caramel out as thinly and quickly as possible.

Using a very sharp knife, cut brittle into 1×2-inch squares.

Let cool completely for 15 minutes and separate the squares.

Rachel Sheff and **Sharon Gomperts, the Sephardic Spice Girls**, share the rich culinary heritage of Middle Eastern and North African Jewish communities through treasured family recipes, social media, writing, and hands-on workshops. Best friends since the age of fifteen, they bring together memory, tradition, and friendship while reconnecting people to the flavors of their grandmothers and inspiring confident, meaningful Sephardic home cooking.

Rachel, born in Casablanca, Morocco, and raised in Los Angeles, learned Moroccan, Spanish, and French cuisine from her mother.

Sharon, born in Tel Aviv to a family with roots in Baghdad and El Azair, Iraq, learned classic Babylonian Jewish dishes from her mother and grandmother.

🌐 www.sephardicspicegirls.com
✉ sephardicspicegirls@gmail.com
📷 @sephardicspicegirls

The Fun Upside-Down & World of AI

BY DR. YAEL MAOZ AND SARA DUNCAN

The world has turned upside down, but it's *Purim*, a perfect time to laugh things off and trust, that *Hashem* has it all worked out.

Last week, Yael asked AI to create a family portrait for her *Purim* card. "I uploaded our photos, typed 'royal Persian family in jewel tones,' and waited."

What came back looked like we'd hired a professional photographer, rented a palace, and achieved the impossible. My daughter wasn't fussing about her shoes matching her outfit. My son was perfectly in sync instead of heading toward a meltdown. My other son was posing nicely instead of giving everyone bunny ears while eyeing the hamantaschen tray.

Nobody was negotiating. Nobody was overstimulated. Everyone looked happy at the exact same moment. A miracle that has never happened in real life.

Venahafoch hu indeed.

Welcome to 2026, where AI has flipped the script on creativity, photography, and how we navigate our overstuffed lives. Just as *Purim* reminds us that sometimes the world needs to be turned on its head to reveal deeper truths, AI is offering new ways to work, create, and maybe even get through *Purim* prep without losing our minds, with smarter planning and a little humor.

THE UNWRITTEN RULES OF USING AI

RULE #1: AI STRUGGLES WITH JEWISH CONTEXT UNTIL YOU TEACH IT.

Ask it to generate "*Purim* costumes" and you'll get generic masquerade balls. But ask for "Queen *Esther* in Persian royal attire inspired by ancient Shushan palace artwork," and suddenly it understands the assignment.

RULE #2: THE 80/20 RULE IS YOUR BEST FRIEND.

AI can get you there most of the way very quickly. The final touches are where your personality and intention come in. Let AI draft a *mishloach manot* poem, then make it yours.

RULE #3: SAVE YOUR BEST PROMPTS LIKE BUBBE'S RECIPES.

When AI finally produces the perfect hamantaschen image, save that prompt. Next year, you'll thank yourself.

RULE #4: AI'S MISTAKES CAN SPARK BETTER IDEAS.

Ask for an "elegant *Purim* table" and you might get pomegranates cascading from a gold crown. Not what you planned, but sometimes more inspiring.

RULE #5: WHEN AI GIVES YOU A SIX-FINGERED MORDECHAI, SCREENSHOT IT.

AI fails are legendary. *Achashverosh* with three arms. *Hamantaschen*, the size of furniture. A grogger that looks suspiciously like a rocket ship. They are funny reminders that AI is a tool, not a replacement.

YOUR PRACTICAL PURIM AI TOOLKIT

A PHOTOGRAPHER'S PERSPECTIVE

As a photographer, a surprising amount of session time is often spent translating ideas. Clients usually know what they want but struggle to describe mood, lighting, or expression, especially when time is limited.

AI helps bridge that gap.

When clients arrive with a clear visual reference created in advance, sessions become more focused and efficient. Lighting decisions are quicker. Posing is clearer. Instead of experimenting, the photographer can move straight into execution. Some clients generate these references using tools like AiFaceSwap.io, which helps them visualize themselves within a setup.

This approach is especially valuable when photographing families navigating sensory sensitivity, ADHD, or special needs. Long sessions with constant adjustments can be overwhelming. A reference image sets expectations early, shortens the shoot, and keeps the experience calmer and more respectful.

From a professional standpoint, AI is not replacing skill. It is a planning tool that improves communication and workflow. Post-production tools like Evoto can then be used efficiently for consistent color correction and subtle refinements.

Clarity before the session creates ease during the process, for photographers and families alike.

HOW TO DO IT:

Use **ChatGPT** or **Claude** and ask: "I'm planning a Purim family photo with two adults and three teens in purple and gold costumes. Suggest pose ideas, lighting, and create a **DALL·E** prompt for each."

Then use **DALL·E**, built into **ChatGPT**, to generate and refine images until you find a direction that feels right.

MISHLOACH MANOT CARDS MADE EASY

Turn your photos into polished cards using **Canva's** AI tools. Upload your image, use Magic Edit to remove backgrounds, type "Persian palace background" into Text to Image, and let Magic Design generate layouts automatically.

Ten minutes from upload to a professional-looking card.

VIDEO GREETINGS THAT WOW

HeyGen creates talking avatar videos with themed backgrounds. Upload a photo, type your message, and send animated greetings.

For something simpler, **CapCut** offers AI stickers and effects like falling *hamantaschen* or sparkles.

THE PRODUCTIVITY PLOT TWIST

AI challenges the assumption that technology removes humanity. When used thoughtfully, it can create more space for it. More time with family. More energy for meaningful work. More room for creativity.

This *Purim*, choose one tool and try it. Generate a reference image. Design a card. Let technology handle the logistics so you can focus on the joy.

After all, in an upside-down world, the most surprising thing might be how much easier it all becomes.

Chag* Purim *Sameach!

Sara Duncan is a personal branding photographer who gives your brand a face that truly represents you. Her relaxed, enjoyable sessions help clients feel confident on camera and create images no AI headshot can replace. She lives in Jerusalem with her husband and three children, and loves yoga and dance.

🌐 **sarafduncan.com**

Dr. Yael Maoz is a publisher and Israel-based entrepreneur working at the intersection of publishing, technology, and storytelling. She is the founder of *Beverly House Press* and a partner in *Weis Living*, and is particularly interested in how emerging tools, especially AI, are reshaping creative work, meaning-making, and modern life.

✉ **yael@beverlyhousepress.com**

LOUD AND CLEAR:

Speaking Up in Your Career

BY HELEN GOTTSTEIN

ESTHER IS TERRIFIED to speak to the king. Which makes sense. It could get her killed.

Look at her starting point. Until she asks a servant what *Mordechai* is doing in a sackcloth in Chapter 3, *Esther* is silent in the book named for her.

One misstep and her life, and those of her people, will be finished. If you've ever had a fear of public speaking, take that and triple it.

Mordechai tells her to go to the king. She says, "It could kill me". In her case, it's literal.

But she does it anyway. *Megillat Esther* is a journey of a woman finding her voice and stepping into her power.

I meet brilliant women with smart ideas, deep knowledge, and industry knowhow who struggle to get heard and even to speak up, even when their lives are not at risk.

HOW ESTHER CAN HELP

As a public speaking consultant, the pre-, during-, and after-speaking anxiety of women can mean endless prep or none at all. It can mean not sleeping for days beforehand. It can mean remaining silent during meeting after meeting and never volunteering to lead a process or speak at regular company events.

And even when they do speak up, some beat themselves up for months afterward over what they wished they'd said or a misspoken word.

They say things like:
I avoid speaking up, even when I knew it would cost me a promotion
I hate the way I sound
Others present and they are all so amazing

So scared that I'll forget what I want to say
They'll think I am an idiot
I'm not smart enough
I'll sound ridiculous
I'll get lost halfway
I always ramble
I think what I know is obvious
I don't want to ask a question and be the only one who doesn't get it
My mouth is so dry I can't get a syllable out

So how does *Esther* do it?

First, she gets support.

She says, I'll go, but I can't do it alone. I want you with me. She asks people to pray for her and fast for her.

Friend, get someone on your team to encourage, push, and cajole you into taking up more space. And if you don't have someone like that, then get on your own team and do it for yourself.

I give a *shiur* on the strategies our *Esther* employs to help her message land, but for now, hear *ye* this.

To all who would want to do it differently, here are three teeny tools that can make a big difference.

Tachlis, how can you speak up more and raise your visibility?

OPEN THE MUTE

Online meetings move fast. If you decide you want to say something, you have to:

Think of the thing
Find the unmute button
Click it

And to goodness, hope what you wanted to say is still relevant. If you're somewhere quiet, open your mic and leave it that way. But remember, it's open.

PREP IN ADVANCE

Stop being surprised that this is the thing being spoken about. Get ready. Make a note or two about what you want to say about a particular agenda item. Even a brief comment is so much better than no comment at all.

USE MUSCULAR LANGUAGE WHEN YOU ARE SURE OF YOUR POSITION.

If you have doubts, that's a whole different ball game. But if you know, speak like you do. Instead of, Maybe, it could be that this could be an idea? Say, It's clear to me that X would work. Here's why. Say, The direction I recommend is X, and give a reason or a data point why that's your recommendation.

• **BONUS POINTS** if you leave your camera open. Want to increase your visibility? Being visible is a fine start.

• **AND IF YOU'VE NOTHING FOR YOURSELF,** take a moment to amplify her. If a colleague says something you think is good, say so. What's lovely about this is karma's a queen.

Compliment someone else and you not only reinforce their voice, you look like the team player you are.

• **AND IF YOU'RE LEADING THE MEETING,** don't let the same three people dominate every single time. Make it part of your agenda to get more women heard more. It sure is mine.

Esther is definitely a hero in that she is afraid and she acts anyway. To all the women who are speaking up even though they are afraid, you are too.

Chag Purim Sameach.

Helen Gottstein, Loud and Clear Training, is a TEDx mentor and keynote coach. She sharpens public speaking skills for corporate teams and people of ambition so they get impact, investments, and applause. She also laughs loudly and regularly burns things in her kitchen. When you're ready to get heard, book your presentation skills and speaking confidence upgrade via her website.

🌐 **loudandcleartraining.com**
✉️ **helen@loudandcleartraining.com**

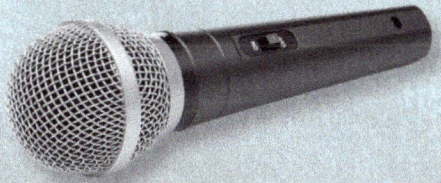

Trust Over Reach:
Collaboration and Influence in the Jewish Digital Space

BY ZAVI (ZAHAVA) SPITZ

Influencers are not a new phenomenon. But within the Jewish world, influence works differently, and understanding that difference matters, especially for nonprofits and mission-driven organizations.

The Jewish digital space is small and deeply interconnected. Audiences overlap, reputations travel quickly, and credibility builds over time. Unlike mainstream influencer campaigns that prioritize reach and scale, Jewish influence operates inside micro-communities such as schools, neighborhoods, life stages, *hashkafic* circles, and shared causes. In this kind of ecosystem, influence is less about visibility and more about responsibility.

This is where many organizations get it wrong. They apply broad influencer strategies to a space that is inherently relational. What works for consumer brands does not always translate when the audience is a community that remembers, talks, and pays attention.

WHY SMALLER CREATORS OFTEN OUTPERFORM

Before going further, it is worth clarifying terminology that is often taken for granted. Nano creators generally have under 2,000 followers, while micro creators typically range from about 2,000 to 10,000 followers. These creators may not see themselves as influencers at all, but they play a critical role in the Jewish digital space.

Unlike large influencers whose content reaches wide and often disconnected audiences, nano and micro creators speak to people they actually know or are closely connected to. Their followers are classmates, neighbors, fellow parents, coworkers, or members of the same community. This proximity is what gives their content weight and why their recommendations often lead to action.

One of the most consistent patterns I see in Jewish influencer marketing is that smaller creators often outperform larger ones. Creators with anywhere from 2,000 to 10,000 followers tend to have more impact, not because they are more authentic, but because of how they function within their communities.

These creators are embedded in specific circles. They have direct, conversational access through comments and DMs. Their followers do not just watch; they respond. When a smaller creator shares an organization, attends an event, or supports a campaign, it often leads to action.

For nonprofits, this distinction is critical. Awareness has value, but action is the real goal. Donations, volunteer sign-ups, and event attendance almost always come from trust built inside smaller, more defined communities.

In practice, the strongest campaigns combine both. A small number of larger influencers help establish visibility and legitimacy, while a wider group of nano and micro creators drive engagement and results. Time and time again, the most meaningful outcomes come from the smallest audiences.

COLLABORATION AS STRATEGY, NOT SENTIMENT

Collaboration is often talked about emotionally, especially in the context of women supporting women. While that language resonates, the real power of collaboration is strategic.

When done correctly, collaboration allows for trust to transfer between audiences. It creates shared credibility and strengthens the overall ecosystem. Rather than relying on one voice or one platform, organizations benefit from being supported across multiple aligned accounts.

For nonprofits, this requires a mindset shift. Influencers are not billboards. They are partners. A successful collaboration starts with clear expectations. An organization should expect awareness and long-term relationship building, not immediate miracles. Influencers, in turn, should approach partnerships with professionalism and clear boundaries. Many creators learn this only after making common early mistakes, such as agreeing to too many collaborations at once, promoting causes or products that are not aligned with their values, or underestimating the time and emotional energy required to represent an organization well.

Clear boundaries mean understanding what you are comfortable sharing, how often you can post, and what expectations you are willing to take on. For women working with influencers, it is equally important to recognize that creators are not volunteers or personal advocates. Respecting their time, expertise, and limits leads to healthier partnerships and far stronger results.

When collaborations are treated as ongoing relationships rather than one-off transactions, their impact grows over time.

WHAT ORGANIZATIONS COMMONLY GET WRONG

Many mission-driven organizations struggle on social media not because their work lacks impact, but because their messaging lacks focus.

One common mistake is having too many faces representing the mission. When content comes from multiple spokespeople, it becomes harder for audiences to build recognition and connection. One or two consistent representatives create clarity and continuity.

Another issue is the absence of narrative continuity. Posting updates without tying them into a larger story weakens engagement. People need to understand how individual moments fit into the broader mission, not just what happened on a given day.

Finally, many organizations expect immediate results. In the Jewish world, influence is relationship-based. Trust is built through repeated exposure and consistent messaging. It rarely happens overnight.

WHAT EFFECTIVE STRATEGY LOOKS LIKE IN PRACTICE

I have seen this firsthand while working with an organization that supports families living below the poverty line. Instead of focusing solely on monthly assistance, the organization highlights vocational training, after-school programs, social workers, and financial guidance, all aimed at helping families achieve long-term stability.

The content that performs best consistently shows the mission in action. A family gaining employment. A child thriving in an after-school program. A tangible outcome tied to donor support. These stories give people a clear understanding of where their involvement makes a difference.

When these stories are shared by aligned micro-creators, parents, educators, and community members connected to the cause,

engagement and donor response increase significantly. People want to feel part of change, and clear storytelling makes that possible.

INFLUENCE COMES WITH RESPONSIBILITY

In the Jewish world, influence carries weight. It shapes opinions, mobilizes communities, and directs resources. Its power does not come from follower count, but from connection and credibility.

When organizations approach influencer strategy with intention, prioritizing community fit, clear storytelling, and long-term relationships, influence becomes more than marketing. It becomes meaningful. And in a community built on shared values and responsibility, that kind of influence has the power to create real change. When handled thoughtfully, Jewish influence does not just amplify messages; it strengthens communities and turns shared values into lasting impact.

Zavi (Zahava) Spitz is the founder and CEO of *Spitz Socialz*, an Israel-based social media agency supporting nonprofits and women-owned businesses. With nearly five years in the social media space, she helps mission-driven brands grow online.

⊙ **@hair.comes.zavi**
⊕ **spitzsocialz.com**
✉ **Zahavaspitz@gmail.com**

www.ingramcontent.com/pod-product-compliance
Lightning Source LLC
Chambersburg PA
CBHW041629140626
46547CB00031B/1948